Fostering
Sustainable
Behavior

Fostering Sustainable Behavior

An Introduction to Community-Based Social Marketing

Doug McKenzie Mohr
and William Smith

NEW SOCIETY PUBLISHERS

for Taryn & Jaime

Cataloguing in Publication Data:
A catalog record for this publication is available from the National Library of Canada.

Cover design by Miriam MacPhail.

Printed in Canada on acid-free, partially recycled (20 percent post-consumer) paper using soy-based inks by Transcontinental/Best Book Manufacturers.
Eighth printing March, 2006.

New Society Publishers acknowledges the financial support of the Government of Canada through the Book Publishing Industry Development Program (BPIDP) for our publishing activities, and the assistance of the Province of British Columbia through the British Columbia Arts Council.

ISBN-10: 0-86571-406-1
ISBN-13: 978-0-86571-406-9

Inquiries regarding requests to reprint all or part of *Fostering Sustainable Behavior* should be addressed to New Society Publishers at the address below.

To order directly from the publishers, please add $4.00 shipping to the price of the first copy, and $1.00 for each additional copy (plus GST in Canada). Send check or money order to:
New Society Publishers
P.O. Box 189, Gabriola Island, B.C. V0R 1X0, Canada

New Society Publishers aims to publish books for fundamental social change through nonviolent action. We focus especially on sustainable living, progressive leadership, and educational and parenting resources. Our full list of books can be browsed on the worldwide web at: http://www.newsociety.com

NEW SOCIETY PUBLISHERS
Gabriola Island, BC, Canada

Education for Sustainability

Fostering Sustainable Behavior is one of New Society Publisher's
Education for Sustainability series of books
copublished with the Academy for Educational Development (AED).
Books in this series focus specifically on strategies for educating
professionals, local officials, activists, and the general public about ways
to promote effective sustainability at all levels:
local, regional, national and international.

AED is an independent, nonprofit organization with 38 years
experience in fostering domestic and global solutions to urgent social,
health, agricultural, and environmental problems.
A recognized leader in social marketing and behavior change theory,
AED has worked in more than 120 countries worldwide, cooperating
with USAID, the World Bank, and other international agencies.

Academy for Educational Development
1825 Connecticut Avenue, NW
Washington, DC 20009-5721, USA
www.aed.org

NEW SOCIETY PUBLISHERS
PO Box 189, Gabriola Island
BC, V0R 1X0, Canada
www.newsociety.com

Contents

Preface

Humanity is at a crossroads. By the end of the next century, global population is expected to reach 11.3 billion.[1] As we move toward a world with twice today's inhabitants, we will be forced to alter our lifestyles dramatically so that our burgeoning population does not outstrip the earth's ability to support humanity and other species. Societies of the future, particularly those in the North, will need to consume far fewer resources and use those resources much more efficiently. Failing to do so will result in what Robert Olson has described as an ecological holocaust.[2]

The movement toward a sustainable future has begun in many places throughout the world. In North America, numerous initiatives to reduce waste, increase energy efficiency, reduce water consumption, and alter transportation patterns are first footholds in the transition to sustainability. This book was written for the people who design these programs. Its purpose is simple: to provide information that can enhance the success of their efforts.

This book details how to uncover the barriers that inhibit individuals from engaging in sustainable behaviors. Further, it provides a set of "tools" that social science research has demonstrated to be effective in fostering behavior change. Each of these tools in and of its own right is capable of having a substantial impact upon the adoption of more sustainable behaviors. Taken together, they provide a powerful set of instruments with which to encourage and maintain behavior change. This book also details how to design and evaluate programs. I refer to the strategies detailed here, and the methods suggested to implement and evaluate them, as "community-based social marketing."

Community-based social marketing draws heavily on research in social psychology which indicates that initiatives to promote behavior change are often most effective when they are carried out at the *community level* and involve *direct contact* with people. The emergence of community-based social marketing over the last several years can be traced to a growing understanding that conventional social marketing, which often relies heavily on media advertising, can be effective in creating public awareness and understanding of issues related to sustainability, but is limited in its ability to foster behavior change.[3,4,5,6]

Community-based social marketing has been shown to be very effective in fostering sustainable behavior

How effective is community-based social marketing in promoting sustainable behavior? In a word, very. For example, compared with the national average, home energy auditors who were trained to use behavior change tools discussed in this book for the largest utility in the United States, Pacific Gas and Electric, persuaded three to four times as many households to weatherize their dwellings.[7] Similarly, when techniques discussed in this book have been used to promote recycling, recycling rates have risen dramatically.[8] Throughout this book you will learn of many other examples in which the methods outlined here have been utilized to effectively promote sustainable behavior.

This book will provide you with the information you need to incorporate community-based social marketing techniques into the programs you design. After reading this book, you will have a new set of tools at your disposal which you can use to create effective community programs to foster sustainable behavior. The first chapter explains why programs that rely heavily on conventional methods to promote behavior change are often ineffective, and introduces community-based social marketing as an attractive alternative for the delivery of programs. Chapter 2 details how to uncover the barriers to sustainable behavior. Chapters 3 through 8 present a variety of tools for overcoming barriers to sustainable behavior. Chapter 9 reviews design and evaluation of a program.

Chapter 10 provides some concluding thoughts on how you can make community-based social marketing work effectively for you. Finally, the appendix "Quick Reference: Community-Based Social Marketing" provides a brief summary of the methods and tools detailed in this book.

In this second edition, we have updated each of the chapters to clarify the concepts they present and have provided, where useful, additional research findings. As well, this edition adds two new chapters, one on the use of incentives and the other a "quick reference" to community-based social marketing. Finally, the second edition is strengthened throughout by the wisdom of my co-author, William Smith, who has extensive experience in the use of social marketing to foster behavior change.

I would like to acknowledge the contributions that many authors have made to the ideas that are expressed in this book. We have been particularly influenced by the writings of Gerald Gardner and Paul Stern, Stuart Oskamp, Deborah Winter, Eliot Aronson and Alan Andreasen. We would also like to acknowledge the contributions that other authors have made to our thinking. A partial listing of these individuals includes: Shawn Burn, Robert Cialdini, Mark Costanzo, John Darley, James Dyal, Scott Geller, Marti Hope Gonzales, William Kempton, Wesley Schultz, Clive Seligman, Neil Wollman, and Ray de Young. You can find references to their work in the references section of the book. You may also find of interest two excellent books. For an in-depth introduction to environmental psychology, see Gerald Gardner and Paul Stern's book, "Environmental Problems and Human Behavior." For a fascinating introduction to social marketing and its application to social change, see Alan Andreasen's "Marketing Social Change."

I would like to acknowledge the people who have assisted me in writing this book. I am grateful to the people who attended workshops I have given on community-based social marketing and sustainability. Your encouragement to write this book, and the suggestions that you made regarding its content, have been very helpful. A number of people have provided me with invaluable feedback. I am grateful to Ben Bennett, Mike Birett, Walter Corson, Adam Ciulini, Elizabeth Crocker, Carla Doucet, Jim Dyal, Jay Kassirer, Glenn Munroe, Glen Pleasance, Linda Varangu, Deborah Du Nann Winter and Neil Wollman for their helpful comments. I would also like to thank my wife, Sue, and my father-in-law, Don McKenzie, for providing me with editorial help with both the first and second editions. I am particularly grateful to the National Round Table on the Environment and the Economy, the Association of Municipal Recycling Coordinators, and the Ontario Ministry of the Environment and Energy for making the publication of the first edition possible. I am also indebted to the Academy for Educational Development (AED), particularly William Smith (my co-author on the second edition) and Brian Day, for their support in making the second edition possible. Finally, I would especially like to thank my wife, Sue, and my young children, Taryn and Jaime, who have been more than understanding, as I took time away from them to write this book.

If you have questions, feedback or additional examples of the tools described in this book, I can be reached at McKenzie@StThomasU.ca.

Doug McKenzie-Mohr
April, 1999

Fostering
Sustainable Behavior

That which is not good for the beehive
cannot be good for the bees.
— *Marcus Aurelius*

When my wife and I (Doug) moved to Fredericton in 1993, we bought a composter for our backyard. During our first summer and fall in our new home we fed the composter diligently. However, by January a snow drift three feet deep stretched from our back door to the composter. I started off the month with good intentions, shoveling a pathway or trampling down the snow with a pair of winter boots that reached nearly to my knees. But by late January, when the temperature dropped to minus 30°F, I had had enough, and despite my good intentions, the organics ended up in the garbage can at the curbside.

My environmental transgressions extend beyond seasonal composting. During the spring, summer and fall I bike to work. However, in the winter, which in Fredericton stretches from November through to early April, I take the taxi. I know that automobiles are a principal source of the carbon dioxide emissions that lead to global warming, so why don't I walk to work or take the bus? To walk to work takes approximately 30 minutes. While the exercise would be good for me, I would rather spend that time with my family. As for the bus, there is no direct bus route from our house to the university — making it slower to take the bus than it is to walk. Finally, the taxi costs only marginally more than bus fare, making it an even easier choice to take the taxi. While I am concerned about the possibility of global warming, my behavior for six months of the year is inconsistent with my concern.

These two anecdotes illustrate the challenges faced in making our communities more sustainable. Composting can significantly reduce the municipal solid waste stream, but only if *people* elect to compost. Mass transit can reduce carbon dioxide emissions, and urban air pollution, but only if *people* leave their cars at home and take the bus or train instead. People play an equally critical role in many other sustainable activities. Programmable thermostats can reduce home heating costs and also carbon dioxide emissions, but only if *people* install and program them. Water efficient toilets and low-flow shower heads can significantly reduce residential water use, but only if *people* have them installed. The purchase of environmentally friendly products can significantly affect our environment, but once again, only if people elect to alter their purchase habits.

Why do some people adopt sustainable activities and others do not? There are many frameworks and theories for explaining human behavior. This book is based on the view that there are generally three explanations for people not engaging in an activity.

- ♦ First, people do not know about the activity (e.g., composting) or its benefits (e.g., significant reductions to the residential waste stream).

- ♦ Second, people who know about the activity may perceive that there are significant difficulties or barriers associated with engaging in it. For example, individuals who know about composting may believe that it is too expensive to purchase a composter, or too inconvenient to compost, or they may be concerned about odors or flies.

- ♦ Third, while people may feel that there are no significant barriers associated with an activity, such as composting, they may perceive that they benefit most from continuing to engage in their present behavior, such as putting organic waste in the garbage, because it is simply easier to do.

To influence what people do, we must understand what they perceive to be the barriers and benefits of an action. Implied in our view of behavior change are three key ideas:

♦ People will naturally gravitate to actions that have high benefits and for which there are few barriers;

♦ Perceived barriers and benefits vary dramatically among individuals. A benefit to one person may be a barrier to another; and finally,

♦ Behavior competes with behavior. That is, people make choices between behaviors. Adopting one behavior (composting) frequently means rejecting another (putting organics in the garbage).

We need, therefore, to understand the perceived barriers and benefits which underlie the behavioral choices that individuals make. Further, if environmental programs are to be effective, we need to be able to deliver programs that remove barriers and enhance benefits for large segments of the population. Community-based social marketing provides the requisite tools to address these two challenges. Community-based social marketers identify the benefits and barriers to behavior and then organize the public into groups, or "segments," which have common characteristics, in order that the delivery of programs can be made most efficient. Central to the development of a community-based social marketing strategy are three questions:

1. What behavior(s) should be promoted? Frequently, it is possible to reach an environmental objective, such as reducing public sector CO_2 emissions or household waste, through a variety of actions. For example, CO_2 emissions can be reduced by encouraging individuals to use mass transit, to insulate their homes, or to install programmable thermostats. Waste reduction can be promoted through source reduction, reuse, recycling or composting. While each of these activities are

worth promoting, usually sufficient resources do not exist to pursue them all. Deciding what behavior(s) to promote should be based primarily on the answer to two questions. First, what is the potential of an action to bring about the desired change? That is, how large of a reduction in CO_2 emissions or the municipal waste stream is achievable through each of the possible actions that might be promoted? Second, what are the barriers and benefits that are associated with each of the potential actions? Deciding which behavior(s) to promote in the end will depend upon not only the potential of an action to bring about the desired change, but also whether the resources exist to overcome identified barriers and enhance perceived benefits.

2. Who should the program address or target? Clearly, a successful program must target those individuals who presently engage in the competing behavior - drive to work, place recyclables in the garbage, water lawns excessively, etc. But effective social marketing also involves identifying who, among those people, is most likely to change, given the barriers and benefits that exist for an alternative behavior being promoted.

3. What conditions will an individual face in deciding to adopt a new behavior? We need to examine closely the conditions which lead individuals to engage in activities we wish to discourage, as well as those which would facilitate the action that we wish to encourage.

These considerations can be represented in a simple matrix (see next page).[1] The vertical axis distinguishes between the barriers and benefits of a behavior, while the horizontal axis compares the target behavior (the behavior we wish people were doing)

	New Behavior	Competing Behavior 1	Competing Behavior 2
Preceived Benefits			
Perceived Barriers			

with its competition (what people are choosing to do instead of the target behavior). The target behavior and the competing behavior(s) both have benefits and barriers. Typically the competing behavior(s) has either more perceived benefits and/or fewer perceived barriers than the target behavior. This is why it is the behavior of choice for many individuals.

The function of a social marketing program, then, is to change the ratio of benefits and barriers so that the target behavior becomes more attractive. There are four non-mutually exclusive ways that this can be done:

♦ Increase the benefits of the target behavior.
♦ Decrease the barriers to the target behavior.
♦ Decrease the benefits of the competing behavior(s).
♦ Increase the barriers of the competing behavior(s).

These possibilities can be more clearly understood by applying them to the example with which we began this chapter. Doug does not walk to work for six months of the year -- instead he takes a taxi.* To understand this behavior better, we need to fill in the

*Shortly after writing this chapter Doug moved to a new home that is significantly closer to work. He now walks to work throughout the year. Also, after his first winter in Fredericton, he moved the composter.

	New Behavior: Walk to work	Competing Behavior 1: Take a Taxi	Competing Behavior 2: Take a Bus in Winter
Preceived Benefits	Helps Environment	Time with Family	Cheaper than Taxi
Perceived Barriers	Lose time with Family	No Alternative Costly Bad for Environment	Loses more time with Family

matrix as shown in the above table. Walking is the target behavior (the behavior we want Doug to adopt) and taking a taxi is the competing behavior (the behavior he is presently performing). Each behavior has benefits and barriers. He reports that the benefits of walking to him are largely environmental and exercise related. Both of these benefits matter, but if he takes the taxi he has another 30 minutes with his family. The time with his family is a benefit that outweighs the environmental and health benefits that accrue from walking. Taking a bus constitutes a third potential competing behavior. We can add it to the matrix and compare the three behaviors from his perspective of barriers and benefits. The environmental benefit to taking the bus is overcome by the added time. He also reports that the financial cost of the taxi is not a barrier as it is only marginally more than the bus fare. Note that his decision to take the taxi is influenced by more than monetary concerns. He has two competing values - environmentalism and family. Neither are financial in nature and both have benefits and barriers. How then can we influence him to change his behavior?

♦ *Educate him.* We could teach him about the environmental

damage caused by the use of the automobile.

- *Increase the barriers he faces to taking a taxi.* We could publicly denounce him as a pseudo-environmentalist, unwilling to make even the smallest sacrifice for the things he says he believes in. Alternatively, we could raise the fares for taking a taxi, making this behavior less financially practical.
- *Decrease the barriers to bus travel.* We could open up a new bus route that was more convenient and saved him time.
- *Increase the benefits of walking.* Look for some way that Doug and his family could walk together -- getting exercise and spending time together as well.
- *Decrease the barriers to bicycle use in winter.* We could invent a new bicycle that is safe to use on icy and snowy streets.
- *Decrease the barriers to walking in winter.* Get Doug to move closer to work so that walking to work in the winter takes less time.

Which of these suggestions would work? Which of these suggestions is possible given the resources we have at our disposal? These are the questions that a community-based social marketing approach can help address. Its primary advantage over many other forms of planning is that it starts with people's behavior and works backward to select a particular tactic suited for that behavior. Too often tactics are selected by the program managers because that is what they know how to do best. Lawyers prefer new regualtions, engineers like new products, educators develop curriculum, and advertisers push the importance of media campaigns. Community-based social marketing argues that for most complex behaviors multifaceted approaches are needed. Further, these approaches will need to change over time. In the

Campaigns that rely solely on providing information often have little or no effect upon behavior

remaining part of this chapter, we will review a few of the most popular tactics and suggest some of their limitations when used in isolation. Finally, we will conclude with an overview of community-based social marketing.

REGULATION

Using the force of law to "regulate" or control behavior is not always popular, but does sometimes work. Auto emissions have decreased significantly because of regulations which forced automobile manufactures to develop, build and market vehicles with lower emissions. Regulating illegal drugs has not been as successful. Twenty years ago it would have been impossible in North America to enforce "No Smoking" policies on airplanes. Today, it is common practice. Our ability to regulate is contingent upon people's willingness to be regulated.

INFORMATION

Information can change behavior. In the area of health promotion, widespread information about heart disease has significantly altered the number of men getting regular check-ups and taking their hypertension medication, resulting in a 50% decline in stroke mortality in the U.S.[2] Information about AIDS has caused a significant increase in the number of adolescents who use condoms, despite numerous experts who felt this change would not take place.[3] Often information interacts with other parts of a social marketing strategy. Information about the importance of wearing condoms was accompanied by new marketing tactics, such as a greater variety of products, more prominent displays, and news items indicating that more young people were using condoms (see Chapter 5 for information on the important role that norms can play in governing behavior). We also know, however, that information alone is often not enough to influence behavior.

Many programs to foster sustainable behavior rely upon large-scale information campaigns. These campaigns are usually based on one of two perspectives regarding changing behavior. The first perspective assumes that changes in behavior are brought about by increasing public knowledge about an issue, such as decreasing landfill capacity, and by fostering attitudes that are supportive of a desired activity, such as recycling. Accordingly, programs based on this perspective attempt to alter behavior by providing information, through media advertising and, frequently, the distribution of brochures, flyers and newsletters.

CHANGING ATTITUDES TO INFLUENCE BEHAVIOR

Is it warranted to believe that by enhancing knowledge, or altering attitudes, behavior will change? Apparently not. Numerous studies document that education alone often has little or no effect upon sustainable behavior. Here are several examples:

♦ In response to the energy crisis of the 1970s, Scott Geller and his colleagues studied the impact that intensive workshops have upon residential energy conservation.[4] In these workshops, participants were exposed to three hours of educational material in a variety of formats (slide shows, lectures, etc.). All of the material had been designed to impress upon participants that it was possible to reduce home energy use significantly. Geller measured the impact of the workshops by testing participants' attitudes and beliefs prior to, and following, the workshops. Upon completing a workshop, attendees indicated greater awareness of energy issues, more appreciation for what could be done in their homes to reduce energy use, and a willingness to implement the changes that were advocated in the workshop. Despite these changes in awareness and attitudes, behavior did not change. In follow-up visits to the homes of 40 workshop participants, only one had followed through on the recommendation to lower the hot water thermostat. Two participants had put insulating blankets around their hot water heaters, but they had done so prior to attending the workshop. In fact, the only difference between the 40 workshop participants and an equal number of non-participants was in the installation of low-flow shower heads. Eight of the 40 participants had installed them, while two of the non-participants had. However, the installation of the low-flow shower heads was not due to education alone. Each of the workshop participants had been given a free low-flow shower head to install.

♦ A study conducted in the Netherlands revealed that providing households with information about energy conservation did not reduce energy use.[5]

♦ High school students who received a six-day workshop that focused on creating awareness of environmental issues were found in a two-month follow-up to be no more likely afterward to have engaged in pro-environmental actions.[6]

♦ Households who volunteered to participate in a ten-week study of water use received a state-of-the-art handbook on water efficiency. The handbook described wasteful water use, explained the relationship between water use and energy consumption, and detailed methods for conserving water in the home. Despite great attention being paid to the preparation of the handbook, it was found to have no impact upon consumption.[7]

The above studies document that information campaigns that emphasize enhancing knowledge or altering attitudes frequently have little or no effect upon behavior. The following studies provide further evidence of the ineffectiveness of this approach. If increasing knowledge and altering attitudes result in behavior change, we should expect measures of attitudes and knowledge to be closely associated with behavior. As shown below, however, there is often little or no relationship between attitudes and/or knowledge, and behavior.

♦ A survey of participants in a voluntary auto emissions inspection revealed that they did not differ in their attitudes toward, or knowledge regarding, air pollution compared to a random sample of individuals who had not had their car inspected.[8]

♦ When some 500 people were interviewed and asked about personal responsibility for picking up litter, 94% acknowledged that individuals bore a responsibility for picking up litter. However, when leaving the interview only 2% picked up litter that had been "planted" by the researcher.[9]

♦ Two large surveys of Swiss respondents found that environmental information, knowledge and awareness were poorly associated with environmental behavior.[10]

♦ In one study, individuals who hold attitudes that are strongly supportive of energy conservation were found to be no more likely to conserve energy.[11]

♦ An investigation of differences between recyclers and non-recyclers found that they did not differ in their attitudes toward recycling.[12]

While environmental attitudes and knowledge have been found to be related to behavior, frequently the relationship is weak or nonexistent. Why would attitudes and knowledge not be more strongly related to behavior? Consider the two anecdotes with which we began this chapter. Doug has attitudes that are supportive of both composting and alternative transportation. Further, he is relatively knowledgeable on both of these topics. Nonetheless, in both cases another factor, inconvenience brought on by winter, moderated whether his attitudes and knowledge were predictive of his behavior. In short, a variety of barriers can deter individuals from engaging in a sustainable behavior. Lack of knowledge and unsupportive attitudes are only two of these barriers.

PROMOTING ECONOMIC SELF-INTEREST

Information-based campaigns are also frequently based on a second perspective. This perspective assumes that individuals systematically evaluate choices, such as whether to install additional insulation to an attic or purchase a low-flow showerhead, and then act in accordance with their economic self-interest. This perspective suggests that in order to affect these decisions, an organization, such as a utility, need only provide information to the public that something is in their financial best interest and consequently the public will behave accordingly. As with information campaigns that focus on altering knowledge and attitudes, efforts that have concentrated on pointing out the financial advantages of a sustainable activity, such as installing a low-flow shower head or adding insulation, have also been largely unsuccessful.[13] Here are two examples:

Few people elect to retrofit their homes in response to economic appeals alone

- ◆ Annually, California utilities spend 200 million dollars on media advertising to encourage energy conservation. These advertisements encourage householders to install energy conserving devices and adopt habits, such as closing the blinds during the day, that will decrease energy use. Despite massive expenditures, these campaigns have had little effect on energy use.[14]
- ◆ In 1978, an act passed by the United States Congress brought into being the Residential Conservation Service (RCS). The RCS mandated that major gas and electric utilities in the United States provide homeowners with on-site assessments in order to enhance energy efficiency. In addition, homeowners had

access to interest-free or low-cost loans and a listing of local contractors and suppliers. In total, 5.6% of eligible households requested that an RCS assessor evaluate their home.[15] Of those who had their home evaluated, 50% took steps to enhance the energy efficiency of their dwelling, compared with 30% for non-participants (the non-participants were households who were on the waiting list to have their homes assessed).[16] What types of actions were taken? In general, the actions were inexpensive and did not involve a contractor. Frequent energy efficiency actions included caulking, weather-stripping, installing clock thermostats, turning down the hot water heater, and installing a hot water heater blanket. These actions reduced energy use per household between 2% and 3%.[17] Given that millions of dollars were spent on the RCS, and that it is possible to reduce residential energy use by more than 50%, an initiative that produces annual savings of 2-3% can only be seen as a failure.

Why did such a comprehensive program fail? In large part the RCS failed because it did not pay adequate attention to the human side of promoting more sustainable energy use. Those who designed this massive initiative assumed that homeowners would retrofit their homes if it was clear that it was in their financial best interest to do so. While this economic perspective does consider the "human" side of sustainable behavior, it does so in a very simplistic way. As a United States National Research Council study concluded, this view of human behavior overlooks "... the rich mixture of cultural practices, social interactions, and human feelings that influence the behavior of individuals, social groups, and institutions."[18]

Information campaigns proliferate because it is relatively easy to distribute printed materials or air radio or television advertising.[19] Advertising, however, is often an extremely expensive way of reaching people. In one distressing case, a California utility spent more money on advertising the benefits of installing insulation in low-income housing than it would have cost to upgrade the insulation in the targeted houses.[20] As Mark Costanzo points out, "Although advertising is an important tool for creating awareness, it is wasteful to invest most of our efforts in an influence strategy that has such a low probability of success."[21]

The failure of mass media campaigns to foster sustainable behavior is due in part to the poor design of the messages, but more importantly to an underestimation of the difficulty of changing behavior.[22] Costanzo and his colleagues note that most mass media efforts to promote sustainable behavior are based on traditional marketing techniques in which the sustainable activity is viewed as a "product" to be sold. Advertising, they note, is effective in altering our preference to purchase one brand over another. But altering consumer preferences is not creating new behavior, rather it involves altering an existing behavior. As they indicate: "These small changes in behavior generally require little expense or effort and no dramatic change in lifestyle (p. 526)." In contrast, encouraging individuals to engage in a new activity, such as walking or biking to work, is much more complex. A variety of barriers to walking or biking to work exist, such as concerns over time, safety, weather, and convenience. The diversity of barriers which exist for any sustainable activity means that information campaigns alone will rarely bring about behavior change.

To date, too little attention has been paid to ensuring that the programs we implement have a high likelihood of actually changing behavior. The cornerstone of sustainability is delivering programs that are effective in changing people's behavior. If we are to make the transition to a sustainable future, we must concern ourselves with what leads individuals to engage in behavior that collectively is sustainable, and design our programs accordingly.

COMMUNITY-BASED SOCIAL MARKETING: AN OVERVIEW

Community-based social marketing is an attractive compliment to regulatory and information intensive campaigns. In contrast to conventional approaches, community-based social marketing has been shown to be very effective at bringing about behavior change. Its effectiveness is due to its pragmatic approach. This approach involves: identifying barriers and benefits to a sustainable behavior, designing a strategy that utilizes behavior change tools, piloting the strategy with a small segment of a community, and finally, evaluating the impact of the program once it has been implemented across a community.

> *The cornerstone of sustainability is delivering programs that are effective in changing people's behavior*

Identifying Barriers and Benefits: If any form of sustainable behavior is to be widely adopted by the public, barriers and benefits to engaging in the activity must first be identified. Community-based social marketers begin, then, by identifying barriers and benefits of an activity. They do so using a combination of community-based research methods.

The barriers they identify may be ***internal*** to the individual, such as lack of knowledge regarding how to carry out an activity (e.g., composting), or ***external***, as in structural changes that need to be made in order for the behavior to be more convenient (e.g., providing curbside organic collection).[23] Community-based social marketers recognize that there may be multiple internal and external barriers to widespread public participation in any form of sustainable behavior and that these barriers will vary for different individuals. For example, personal safety is more likely to be a concern to women as they consider using mass transit than it is for men. In contrast to the two perspectives just discussed, community-based social marketers attempt to remove as many of these barriers as possible.

Practitioners of community-based social marketing further appreciate that a different constellation of barriers and benefits will exist for different activities (e.g., recycling, composting, alternative transportation). Social science research indicates that the barriers that prevent individuals from engaging in one form of sustainable behavior, such as adding insulation to an attic, often have little in common with the barriers that keep individuals from engaging in other forms of sustainable behavior, such as recycling.[24] Further, this research demonstrates that even within a class of sustainable activities, such as waste reduction, very different barriers emerge as being important.[25] That is, different barriers exist for recycling, composting, or source reduction.

Since the barriers that prevent individuals from engaging in sustainable behavior are activity specific, community-based social marketers begin to develop a strategy only after they have identified a particular activity's barriers. Once these barriers have been identified, they develop a social marketing strategy to remove them and/or enhance the perceived benefits of engaging in the activity.

Behavior Change Tools: Social science research has identified a variety of "tools" that are effective in changing behavior. These tools include such approaches as gaining a commitment from an individual that they will try a new activity, such as taking household hazardous waste to a collection depot, or developing community norms that encourage people to behave more sustainably. The techniques that are used by community-based social marketers are carried out at the community level and frequently involve direct personal contact. Personal contact is emphasized because social science research indicates that we are most likely to change some behaviors in response to direct appeals or social support from others.

Piloting: Prior to implementing a community-based social marketing strategy, it is piloted in a small portion of a community. Given the high cost of implementing many programs, it is essential to know that a strategy will work before it is implemented on a large scale. Conducting a pilot allows a program to be refined until it is effective. Further, a pilot allows alternative methods for carrying out a project to be tested against one another and the most cost-effective method to be determined. Finally, conducting a pilot can be a crucial step in demonstrating to funders the worthiness of implementing a program on a broad scale.

Evaluation: The final step of community-based social marketing involves ongoing evaluation of a program once it has been implemented in a community.

In conducting an evaluation, community-based social marketers emphasize the direct measurement of behavior change over less direct measures such as self reports or increases in awareness. The information gleaned from evaluation can be used to refine the marketing strategy as well as provide evidence that a project should receive further funding.

The following chapters detail these four steps of community-based social marketing. Chapter 2 presents how to identify barriers and benefits to an activity. Chapters 3 through 8 introduce a variety of behavior change tools and provide advice on how to incorporate them into a program. Chapter 9 explains how to design a strategy and conduct a pilot, as well as how to evaluate a program in a cost-effective way once it has been implemented across a community. After reading these chapters, you will have the information you need to create programs that can have a substantial impact on the adoption of sustainable behavior in your community.

2

Uncovering
Barriers and Benefits

*Don't let us forget that the causes of human actions
are usually immeasurably more complex than
our subsequent explanations of them.*
— *Fyodor Dostoevsky*

We each have hunches about why people engage in activities such as walking to work, recycling or composting. For instance, theories regarding personal motivations for recycling abound. Recycling, it has been suggested, is popular because it serves to alleviate our guilt for not making the more difficult and inconvenient changes toward sustainable living. This hypothesis suggests that curbside recycling is simply an antidote to the guilt we feel when, for example, just after placing our recycling container at the curb, we hop into our own personal global warming factory and head off to work. Other theories suggest that individuals recycle because it is convenient, those around us recycle, it makes us feel good about ourselves, or we are simply badgered into it by our children.

Hunches regarding what motivates people to engage in sustainable behavior are important. These personal theories need to be identified for what they are, however: simply speculation. Speculation regarding what leads individuals to engage in responsible environmental behavior should never be used as the basis for a community-based social marketing plan. Prior to designing such a plan you need to set aside personal speculation and collect the information that will properly inform your efforts.

To create an effective community-based social marketing strategy, you must be able to sort through the competing theories and discover the actual barriers that inhibit individuals from engaging

19

in the activity you wish to promote. In addition, you need to uncover what benefits people believe are associated with engaging in the activity. Once you have this information, you are well positioned to create an effective strategy. The purpose of this chapter, then, is to introduce methods for uncovering barriers and benefits.

THREE STEPS FOR UNCOVERING BARRIERS AND BENEFITS

Uncovering barriers and benefits involves three steps. You want to begin by reviewing relevant articles and reports. Following this review, qualitative research involving focus groups and observational studies is conducted to explore in-depth the attitudes and behaviors of community residents regarding the activity. Building on the information obtained from qualitative research, a survey is then conducted with a random sample of residents. A survey can greatly enhance knowledge of the barriers and benefits for the behavior you wish to promote. If you have a consultant doing this research for you, it is wise to ask for an interim report at the end of these three steps in which information gleaned from the literature review is presented, results of the focus groups, observation, and survey are detailed, and promising social marketing strategies based on this research are identified.

For organizations that typically have research done by consultants, this chapter is meant to provide information against which you can scrutinize proposals. If you are likely to do this work internally, this chapter will provide you with sufficient information to set out a clear research strategy. When combined with additional reading, this chapter will provide you with enough information to conduct your research in-house.[1]

1. Literature Review

Since the barriers and benefits for a sustainable behavior are activity specific (see Chapter 1), the first step in designing a community-based social marketing strategy is to review relevant articles and reports. Prior to conducting your literature review, you should be clear on your mandate. If your position involves promoting mass transit over driving, then your literature search is already well defined. However, if you have a broad mandate, such as promoting residential energy or water conservation, to expedite your search you will need to clarify your mandate further before proceeding. Residential energy conservation, for example, can include behaviors as diverse as weather-stripping, adding additional insulation, installing clock thermostats, closing and opening windows, installing compact fluorescent bulbs, or planting trees.

Conducting a Literature Search

There are four sources of information that you will want to tap into for your literature search.

♦ Thumb through trade magazines and newsletters for related articles. Often these articles are summaries of more extensive reports and can be good leads for where to search for in-depth information.

♦ You will want to find out what reports have been written on the topic by other communities. These reports are often difficult to obtain but are well worth the effort. Begin by contacting organizations that act as information clearinghouses for the behavior you wish to promote. For example, contacting the United States National Recycling Coalition, the Recycling Council of Ontario, or the Waste Watch Centre, can be invaluable if you are designing a waste reduction initiative.[2] If a relevant clearinghouse does not exist, call several well-connected individuals to trace down reports that have been prepared for other organizations.

Take the time to contact the authors of reports or articles that are of particular interest to you

♦ Search the databases of your local or closest university for related academic articles. Many of the articles that will be of interest to you can now be found by electronically searching databases. When you conduct these searches, pay particular attention to recent review articles that synthesize the current state of knowledge on the topic. If you have access to the internet you may wish to check the web site that I (Doug) have set up (www.cbsm.com). At this site you will find a searchable database of academic articles on fostering sustainable behavior. You can search this database by behavior and/or the behavior change tools described in subsequent chapters. The website also contains a discussion forum where you can exchange ideas and ask questions of others who are involved in designing programs and/or conducting research in a particular area.

♦ Once you have reviewed the reports and academic articles that you have found, call the authors of studies that are of particular interest. Often these individuals will have pre-press publications that you will not be able to find elsewhere. Further, they may currently be engaged in research that can inform your efforts. Academics can be a particularly useful resource for tracking down research articles and reports that you may have missed in your previous searches. Mention the studies you have found and ask if there are other studies of which you should be aware. Often they will be willing to fax you a listing of relevant articles. Finally, ask if you can call back at a later point in your project to obtain further advice. Cultivating a good relationship with an academic who works in your area can assist you not only with keeping abreast of current literature, but also with issues related to analyzing your survey data and designing and evaluating your project.

Finally, if you are having the literature search done by consultants, ask that they search for relevant information in each of these four areas.

2. Qualitative Research

Two forms of qualitative research can be particularly useful in identifying barriers and benefits - observational studies and focus groups.

Observational Studies

Observational studies involve watching individuals carry out a desired behavior in settings that are as natural as possible. Since behavior is observed directly, this technique sidesteps the inherent limitations of asking people about their behavior. Often when individuals are questioned via a focus group or a survey, their self-

---

OBSERVATIONAL EXAMPLE: RECYCLING IN A PUBLIC AREA

At four sites adjacent to the Washington and Lincoln Memorials in Washington, D.C., an area popularly known as the Mall, the recycling behavior of individuals was studied[3] Three of the four sites had an elaborate sign indicating what items could be recycled (glass bottles, plastic bottles, foam cups and containers, and aluminum cans). To make recognition of the items that could be recycled easy, each of these items was visually depicted. In addition, the sign had a picture of two young children using the provided recycling container. Finally, the sign included information on recycling and indicated the amount of garbage that was produced each week on the Mall. All four sites had recycling containers which had printed on them the recycling symbol and the words: Plastic, Glass, Aluminum only. To distinguish the trash container from the recycling container, it was of a different size and shape and had printed on it the words: Trash Only. These four sites also differed with respect to how busy they were and how close they were to a concession stand. It was expected that the presence of the elaborate signs and clearly marked recycling containers would lead to high levels of recycling and very little contamination (recyclables placed in the trash container and vice versa) relative to the site

... more ...

---

reports exaggerate the extent to which they engage in an activity, such as recycling. Observation is also useful in determining what triggers or cues a particular behavior and what reinforces or supports it. Observation can also detect important skill deficits that are overlooked by individuals when they self-report their performance. For example, individuals asked about their ability to install a programmable thermostat or weather stripping may incorrectly assess their skill at these activities. Observational research can be conducted in several ways.

With performance observation, a comparison is made between

that had only the containers. Teams of trained observers were used to record how people disposed of their trash and recyclables. Further, these observers also sorted the garbage to determine actual recycling and contamination rates.

Surprisingly, the three sites which contained the elaborate signs were no more effective at inducing correct disposal of recyclables and garbage than was the site without the sign. Further, there were high levels of contamination at all four sites.

Observations of people's recycling behavior clearly indicated that the signs were being ignored, despite the fact that they were well-designed and well-placed. After extensive discussion among the observers, several possible explanations arose for the surprising results. First, the observers considered who comes to the Mall. The majority of individuals on the Mall are visitors who wish to spend their time at the attractions the Mall provides. With so much to see and do, few visitors, they concluded, could be bothered with reading an elaborate sign or paying attention to the labels on the cans. This conclusion was supported by the observations that were made — very few of the visitors attended to the sign. Second, it was believed that the signs could be simplified and more clearly distinguish

... more ...

how an activity should be carried out and how individuals actually carry it out. For example, how individuals compost can be compared to how they should ideally compost. This form of observation is useful when the behavior to be observed is well understood and the correct carrying out of the behavior is essential to achieving the best results. Performance observation is useful in determining needed skills and common errors that people make.

Narrative observation is particularly useful when the researcher is unfamiliar with how a person engages in a particular behavior.

---

between the trash and recycling containers. Finally, it was suggested that in order to improve substantially the disposal of recyclables and garbage, the assistance of the sales staff at the concession booths would have to be sought. This suggestion highlights the need to develop community-based social marketing strategies that carefully target segments of the public. The observations conducted in this study demonstrated that very little of the material deposited was recyclable, and most of the recyclable material had been purchased at a concession stand. To target more directly people with recyclable material, concession stand staff could be asked to provide a simple verbal prompt (see chapter 4 on prompts) to those customers who purchase a recyclable container. In return, the concession stands would be provided with a small financial reward on those days when an agreed upon recycling goal is met.

This example illustrates how important actual observation can be. In this project, observation allowed the researchers to conclude that few visitors were attending to the sign and that most recyclables were purchased at one of the concession stands. Accordingly, they were able to devise a social marketing strategy that took into account these two observations.

Here performance is not well understood and the goal is to determine what people do. In Egypt, for example, researchers were unfamiliar with how garbage was placed in the local irrigation system. A narrative observation was used to record the times of day, the frequency and who was dumping trash into the canals. The researchers discovered that women and not men, as originally believed, were the largest polluters. This information led to a social marketing strategy that was very different from what had been originally contemplated.

Avoid sending information packages prior to conducting focus groups. If you provide information prior to running the focus groups your participants will no longer be representative of your community.

Other observational techniques include behavioral audits, frequency observations, and duration observations. With behavioral audits, compliance is assessed. This technique is useful to assess, for example, the extent to which people are correctly separating recyclables from garbage. Frequency observations involve determining how often a somewhat rare behavior occurs, while duration observation is used when a behavior may occur occasionally although it is necessary for the behavior to occur far more frequently.

Observational strategies have several advantages over other approaches. First, because these strategies are based upon direct observation, the information obtained is more reliable than information obtained from self-reports. Second, the very nature of conducting an observational study allows an understanding of people's performance of the behavior that is difficult, if not impossible, to obtain in any other way. However, observational studies are difficult to do on a large scale and do not replace focus groups and surveys as methods of determining the perceived benefits and barriers of an activity.

Focus Groups

The literature review and observations of individuals directly engaging in the activity will assist in identifying issues to be explored further with residents of your community through focus groups. A focus group consists of six to eight community residents who have been paid to discuss issues that your literature review has identified as important (when focus group participants are volunteers there is a strong likelihood that they are participating because they have a greater interest in the topic than others in the community). The participants for the focus groups are usually randomly chosen from the community. To select the participants, simply choose randomly phone numbers from the phone book. When contacting the potential participants, be sure to let them know how their names were selected. To ensure a good rate of participation, make it convenient for people to participate. Arranging transportation and childcare can significantly increase participation rates. Remember, you want your focus group participants to be as representative of the community as possible. The more barriers that you remove to participating, the more representative your focus groups will be.

Focus groups provide an opportunity to discuss in-depth the perceptions and present behaviors of community residents relevant to the activity you are planning to promote. To maximize what you can learn from the focus group, you should come to the meeting with a set of clearly defined questions that have been informed by your literature review. You will want to begin the session by informing the participants that they were chosen at random to provide your organization with information about the relevant behavior. You will also want to reassure them that there are no right or wrong answers for the questions that you will be asking them and that what you are most interested in is their perceptions. You will want to remind them that their responses are confidential. Since you will be steering the conversation through the set of questions that you have created, you will want to have a co-worker act as a note taker.

As the facilitator for the discussion it is important that you establish a supportive but firm role with the attendees. It is not unusual to have one or two members of a focus group attempt to monopolize the discussion and in so doing make other members feel that their comments are not important. Your role is to facilitate in such a way that less assertive members, or individuals who might have differing views, feel comfortable in speaking out. Prior

---

EXAMPLE: WHAT QUESTIONS MATTER?

The questions that you ask in your focus groups should be informed by the literature search that preceded it. For example, research on composting suggests that several factors distinguish householders who compost from those who do not. Householders who do not compost are likely to perceive composting as an unpleasant activity that may involve unwanted odours in the house or backyard. Further, they are likely to associate composting with attracting unwanted animals or insects. In addition, they are likely to perceive that they have insufficient time to compost, and believe that composting is inconvenient. In contrast, those who compost have been found to be strongly motivated to reduce waste, gain personal satisfaction from "doing their part," and appreciate the benefits to their garden that compost provides.

Building on these research findings, it would be useful to conduct at least four focus groups. Two of the focus groups would include only non-composters, while the other two focus groups would involve only composters.

SAMPLE QUESTIONS FOR NON-COMPOSTERS:

1. Would each of you please describe the single most important reason why you don't compost?

... more ...

to conducting your first focus group you will need to be comfortable with statements such as "I have received some very informative feedback from you, now I would like to hear what others have to say," and "I understand that you feel strongly about this issue, but I also know that some people have very different views on this matter, would anyone like to share them?" These statements assure participants that even if there are some belligerent or overly talkative members, you are ensuring that views of other members will be heard.

---

2. Some people think of composting as unpleasant. Is that a perception that each of you shares? If so, what do you see as unpleasant about composting?
3. Do you have any ideas regarding what could be done to make composting less unpleasant?
4. How convenient do you believe it is to compost?
5. What would make composting more convenient?
6. What else would you like to tell me about composting?

SAMPLE QUESTIONS FOR COMPOSTERS:
1. Would each of you please describe the single most important reason why you compost?
2. Some people think of composting as unpleasant. Is that a perception that each of you shares?
3. For those of you who do not see composting as unpleasant, did you at one time see it as an unpleasant activity? If so, what has changed your perception of composting?
4. What suggestions can you give me regarding how composting can be presented in our community as a more pleasant activity?
5. People who do not compost often describe it as inconvenient. Are there suggestions that you have regarding how you have made composting convenient?

Remember that you are interested in people's views unadulterated by any information that you might present in your subsequent program. Therefore, avoid sending information packages prior to conducting focus groups (handing them out afterward is fine). If you provide information prior to running the focus groups, your participants will no longer be representative of your community.

When the focus groups are completed, you will want to summarize the comments that have been made. One effective technique is to tabulate the number of times that a specific comment was made, or agreed with, by members of the focus group. In general, you should pay close attention to comments that are made frequently (e.g., "I would compost, if I could be assured that it would not attract rodents").

3. Survey

Focus groups are an essential step in enhancing your understanding of how community residents view the behavior you wish to promote. However, by themselves focus groups do not provide sufficient information upon which to base a social marketing plan. Focus groups are limited by the small number of participants, the impact that members of the focus group have upon one another, and the qualitative nature of the answers obtained. The small number of participants makes generalizing the results to the larger community unwise and, while interviewing participants in groups is cost-effective, members of a focus group can have a substantial effect on what opinions are expressed. Further, the qualitative data obtained in focus groups places considerable limits on the types of analyses that can be performed. Despite these limitations, focus groups provide valuable information about what issues residents see as important and also how they speak about the topic. As such, focus groups will help enrich your understanding of the activity you wish to promote, and ensure that a more comprehensive survey will be well constructed and that questions contained in the survey will be readily understood by the respondents.

Several methods are available for obtaining reliable information on the current beliefs and behaviors of community residents regarding the activity you wish to promote. These methods are person-to-person interviews, a mailed survey, and a phone survey. Person to person interviews include both lengthy in-depth interviews plus shorter more targeted intercept interviews. The latter is particularly helpful to validate information obtained from focus groups. Imagine that a few focus group members suggest that men really believe that recycling is for women. How prevalant is this belief? An intercept interview could be organized (perhaps in a mall, at a gas station, or sporting events) to ask just a few questions targeted at this specific belief. This type of survey can be completed quickly, at low cost and provide invaluable support to a broad strategy or approach.

In-depth personal interviews are capable of providing reliable and detailed information, however, they suffer from two significant limitations; they are expensive to conduct and take a considerable amount of time to complete. To conduct in-depth person-to-person interviews, a random sample of residences would first be selected. Next, each of these homes would be mailed a letter introducing the purpose of the interview to them. Each household would then be called and, if willing, a time for an interview would be arranged. Paid interviewers would then travel to each home to conduct the interview. While this detailed process is occasionally warranted, conducting person-to-person interviews usually is an inefficient use of your resources.

In contrast, a mailed survey is much less expensive to conduct and the entire survey can be completed in a reasonable amount of time. However, mailed surveys have a major drawback: the number of people who will complete and return the survey, or what is referred to as the response rate, is often between 20% and 40%. Such a low response rate brings into serious question the repre-

SAMPLE COMPOSTING SURVEY QUESTIONS

1. Composting involves a variety of steps. These steps include collecting food scraps and yard waste, placing these materials in an outside compost bin, mixing the compost on a regular basis, and emptying the compost bin and applying the finished compost to a garden or flower bed.

   Does your household compost?   ☐ Yes ☐ No

   IF THE HOUSEHOLD COMPOSTS, THEN READ "A" BELOW. IF THEY DO NOT COMPOST, THEN READ "B" BELOW.

   A. With these steps in mind, we would like to ask you to respond to the following statements. Please rate these statements on a six-point scale, where "1" is "strongly disagree" and "6" is "strongly agree."

   B. While we understand that you do not compost, please respond to the following statements based on what you "believe" it would be like to compost, rather than what you have actually experienced. Please rate these statements on a six-point scale, where "1" is "strongly disagree" and "6" is "strongly agree."

	strongly disagree				strongly agree		D/K
• It is inconvenient to collect food scraps in the kitchen	1	2	3	4	5	6	7
• Collecting food scraps in the kitchen produces unwanted odors	1	2	3	4	5	6	7
• Collecting food scraps in the kitchen attracts flies	1	2	3	4	5	6	7
• It is inconvenient to take food scraps out to the compost bin	1	2	3	4	5	6	7

2. IF THE HOUSEHOLD COMPOSTS, THEN READ "A" BELOW. IF THEY DO NOT COMPOST, THEN READ "B" BELOW.

A. Thinking of the reason why your household composts, rate the importance of the following reasons on a six-point scale where "1" is "not at all important" and "6" is "very important."

B. Please rate the following reasons on how important they would be in encouraging you to begin composting. Please rate these statements on a six-point scale, where "1" is "not at all important" and "6" is "very important."

	not at all important				very important		D/K
• save money by decreasing the need for store bought fertilizers 1	2	3	4	5	6	7
• reduce the amount of waste generated by our household 1	2	3	4	5	6	7
• the development of a nutrient-rich soil............1	2	3	4	5	6	7
• feelings of satisfaction from composting 1	2	3	4	5	6	7
• the cost of the compost unit 1	2	3	4	5	6	7

sentative nature or generalizability of the findings. Given the inconvenience of completing and mailing the survey, individuals who participate are likely more interested in your topic than those who elect not to participate. As a result, participants in a mailed survey provide an unrealistic picture of community attitudes and behavior.

Phone surveys have several advantages over mailed surveys

and person-to-person interviews. First, compared with a mailed survey, it is possible to obtain a much higher response rate, providing a more accurate assessment of current community attitudes and behavior. While it is possible to obtain a much higher response rate, clearly not everyone will agree to participate. However, those individuals who choose not to participate can be asked to complete a brief refusal survey. A refusal survey consists of three to four questions that are also found in the complete survey (e.g., does your household compost). Further, the refusal survey normally takes no longer than half a minute to complete. Because the refusal survey is so brief, individuals who wish not to participate in the full survey frequently agree to complete the briefer refusal survey. By comparing responses of refusal survey participants with those of full survey participants, potential differences between participants and non-participants can be explored. If no differences exist between the two sets of responses, the results of the full survey can be more reliably generalized back to your community. If differences do appear, greater caution is warranted in generalizing the results.

In addition to providing a higher response rate than a mailed survey and the opportunity to conduct a refusal survey, phone surveys are less expensive to conduct and can be completed in a much shorter amount of time than can person-to-person interviews.

Additional advantages of phone surveys include:

♦ Random-digit dialling of community residents is possible (ensures a random sample of community residents).
♦ Phone access to otherwise difficult-to-reach populations is possible (e.g., high rise apartments, rural households).
♦ Phone surveys are relatively easy to staff and manage. Compared with personal interviews, fewer staff are needed, the staff need not be near the sample geographically, and supervision and quality control are easier.

What to Ask About?

Observational approaches, focus groups and surveys all rely upon different approaches for collecting information. But each approach has a basic set of questions that it is trying to address. These questions are grounded in theory and research in the social sciences. [4] Based upon this work we have developed a set of six questions which can be adapted to a variety of behaviors to identify key determinants, or influences upon behavior. For each of the following questions replace "X" with the behavior you are interested in promoting.

Barriers

1. What makes it difficult to do X?
2. What makes it easy to do X?

Benefits

3. What positives are associated with doing X?
4. What negatives are associated with doing X?

Social Norms

5. Who wants you do X, and how much do you care about their opinion?
6. Who doesn't want, or care if you do X, and how much do you care about their opinion?

Seven Steps in Creating a Survey

Items to include in your survey will be guided by your literature review and the focus groups. But how do you begin to write the survey? Writing a well-constructed survey takes time and patience. Here are some guidelines to make that process easier.

Step One: Clarify your Objective

Begin by writing a simple paragraph that describes what the survey is meant to accomplish. This paragraph has two purposes. First, it will force you to be clear on what the survey is to measure. Second, once you have it completed, you can show it to others involved in the project. You will be spending considerable time writing, conducting and analyzing the data from the survey. You want to make sure, before you begin this process, that those who have a stake in the results are all onboard regarding what the survey is to accomplish.

Following the example that we have used throughout this chapter, imagine that you are designing a community-based social marketing strategy for composting. You have two purposes: 1) To encourage people who are presently not composting to begin, and 2) To encourage seasonal composters to compost throughout the year. Given this background, your objective statement might read something like this:

Note that the objective paragraph for the survey indicates that there are two purposes, one of which is more important than the

---

Sample Objective Statement
This survey's primary purpose is to determine what factors distinguish year-round composters from individuals who never compost. A secondary purpose is to determine which factors distinguish year-round composters from seasonal composters.

---

other. Giving priorities to different objectives of a survey can assist you later in deciding how many questions to devote to each task that the survey is to perform. Also note that comparisons between three groups are called for. In other words, your sample will need to contain three groups: year-round composters, non-composters and seasonal composters.

Step Two: List Items to Be Included
Once you are happy with your "survey objective statement," the next step is to create a list of items that "might" be included in the

survey. Note that at this time you are not concerning yourself with writing questions, only with determining the "themes" that will be covered in the questionnaire. Most of the items on your list should come from what you have learned from your literature review and from your focus groups. Once you have created a comprehensive list, organize it into logical groupings. Place items related to behavior together, group attitude items together and similarly group demographic topics.† Finally, once you have grouped the items on your list, you are ready to check each item against your "survey objective paragraph." You want to determine for each item on your list if it furthers the purpose of your survey. In other words, does it help to determine any of the goals laid out in your objective statement? If it doesn't, it should be eliminated. When you have your list finalized, you are ready to begin writing the survey.

Step Three: Write the Survey

In writing the survey, you will want most, if not all, of your questions to be closed-ended. Open-ended items are difficult to analyze and greatly extend the length of your survey. Keep in mind that you will want to be able to complete your whole survey in 10 minutes or less. To be able to ask as many questions as possible in a short amount of time, you will want to use only a few types of scales in your survey.

Note that in the following survey, each of the scales has six points plus a "D/K" or "don't know" option. Six or seven point scales are preferable to three, four or five point scales, in that they provide for a broader range of answers. Having a broader range is important, when most people are likely to be clustered at one end of the

---

† As you develop your survey keep in mind that activities, such as composting, are made up of a variety of behaviors (collecting food waste in a kitchen container, placing food waste in a composter, placing yard waste in a composter, stirring the compost, etc). To understand fully the barries to an activity, make sure that your survey asks questions about each of the behaviors that make up the activity.

scale or the other. It is likely, for example, that on a four point scale most people would respond with a "3" or "4" regarding how frequently they recycle glass and food cans. However, when the scale is expanded to six items, answers will be more dispersed. Whether you use a six or seven point scale will depend upon whether you wish to provide respondents with a midpoint. Using an odd-numbered scale provides a midpoint that allows respondents who are divided in how to respond to select this option. However, the midpoint may also be selected by respondents who are unsure of how to answer. Whichever option you select, stay with it throughout the survey, to avoid confusion for respondents.

Note also that only the endpoints are spelled out for each scale (e.g., in question #1 "1-never" and "6-all the time"). Providing just the endpoints lessens the length of time that it takes to read the sur-

---

Questions about Questions

1. Is this a question that can be asked exactly as written?
2. Is this a question that will mean the same thing to everyone?
3. Is this a question that people can answer?
4. Is this a question that people will be willing to answer?

---

vey to the participants. Further, it allows you to assume that the distance between each of the items on the scale (e.g., 4 to 5) is equal. If you provide labels for each of the items on the scale, the respondent can no longer infer that the distance between each of the items is equivalent. For example, we understand that the distance between 5 and 6 is equal to the distance between 4 and 5. However, we can't assume equivalence with labels (e.g., Is the distance between "6-strongly agree" and "5-moderately agree" the same as the distance between "5-moderately agree" and "4-mildly agree" ?). Because the distance between the scale items is no longer equivalent when you apply labels, there are more limitations placed on how you can subsequently analyze the data.

Finally, note that instructions to the surveyor are typed in capital letters to distinguish them from what is to be read to the respondent.

You should not have to write the whole survey yourself. You may wish to include questions that were part of other surveys (just seek permission before doing so). Further, you can use the demographics items in other surveys as guides for your demographic section (a standard set of demographic questions is provided at the website www.cbsm.com in the online chapter on uncovering barriers and benefits).

Finally, as you write your survey, you will want to ask the above four questions of each question in your survey.

Step Four: Pilot the Survey

Once the survey has been written, pilot it with 10 to 15 residents. During the pilot, the wording and order of questions in the survey can be scrutinized. Questions that respondents find confusing or difficult to answer can be rewritten before the full survey is conducted. Further, the pilot ensures that each survey can be conducted in under 10 minutes.

Miscalculations regarding the length of time that it takes to contact respondents or complete the survey can be very costly when it comes time to conduct the survey. Your pilot will help you to ascertain that your budget is realistic. Do not include the data you obtain from the pilot with the data you obtain from the actual survey.

Step Five: Select the Sample

Once you have completed the pilot and made whatever revisions are necessary, you are ready to obtain your sample. At this point you have two options. First, you may decide to have the survey completed by a survey research firm. Prices vary significantly, so shop around, but you can expect to pay at least $20 U.S. for each survey completed (in 1997 dollars). This price should include all charges, including conducting the survey, the refusal survey, and entering the data into a spreadsheet for data analysis.

If you decide to conduct the survey yourself, you may wish to have a firm provide you with a list of randomly derived residential phone numbers and addresses for your community. How many people should you sample? There is no easy answer to this question and here is where cultivating a good relationship with an academic working in the field can be of assistance. The size of the sample and how it is obtained will determine how confident you can be in your results. However, there is one other issue that will determine the sample size needed. Certain types of statistical analyses require a minimum number of participants for each barrier investigated (usually 10 to 12). Therefore, if you are designing a survey to look at composting, and you have 20 different barriers that you wish to explore simultaneously, you will need to complete roughly 200 surveys (20 X 10).

Step Six: Conduct the Survey

If you are doing the survey "in-house," you will need to train the people who will be conducting the survey. At the website (www.cbsm.com) you can find a set of instructions for interviewers (these instructions are in the online chapter on uncovering barriers and benefits).

Step Seven: Analyze the Data

Many of the current statistical packages, such as the Statistical Package for the Social Sciences (SPSS) make analyzing data much easier than it was even a few years ago. Obtaining descriptive statistics, frequencies, and comparing means is now as simple as pulling down a menu and selecting the variables and analysis that you want. Gone are the days in which you had to write complex computer instructions to analyze data. The result is that basic statistics are now within reach of virtually everyone. However, you will want to go beyond obtaining the means and frequencies to lay the groundwork for your community-based social marketing campaign.

If you glance back at the survey objective statement, you will notice that the survey had two purposes: distinguishing between composters and non-composters; and distinguishing between year-round composters and those who compost seasonally. To answer these two questions requires multivariate statistics; such as multiple regression, discriminant analysis or logistic regression. Multivariate statistics allow you to determine the factors that distinguish householders who compost from those who do not, and also enables you to analyze the relative importance of these factors. For example, a recent study that I (Doug) conducted with a former student, Laurie Beers, utilized discriminant analysis and revealed the following five factors were most important in distinguishing year-round composters from non-composters. [5] Note that these factors are presented in order of importance:

◆ Those who composted reported a greater desire to reduce the amount of waste they produced than did non-composters.

◆ Non-composters perceived composting to be a more unpleasant activity than those who composted (e.g., they associated it with unpleasant odors, flies, rodents).

◆ Composters perceived the activity to be more convenient than did those who did not compost.

◆ Those who did not compost believed that they did not have the time to compost.

◆ Composting households reported recycling glass and cans

more frequently.

Knowing which factors are most important in distinguishing individuals who have adopted a sustainable behavior from those who have not is an essential first step in developing a communi-

Knowing which factors are most important in distinguishing individuals who have adopted a sustainable behavior, from those who have not, is an essential first step in developing a community-based social marketing strategy.

ty-based social marketing strategy. The above results provide a clear indication of some of the barriers that would need to be surmounted to encourage more people to compost. For example, perceptions that composting is unpleasant, inconvenient and involves a significant investment of time are important issues that a community-based social marketing strategy would need to address.

Analyzing the data using multivariate statistical techniques is an essential aspect in the development of a sound marketing strategy. Less sophisticated statistical approaches such as calculating means or correlations are limited in their ability to provide information on the relative importance of the factors that lead individuals to engage in the behaviors of interest to you. Unless you or someone else in your organization has a background in statistics, you will want to obtain assistance at this point. Many graduate students are trained in multivariate statistics and with a few phone calls you should be able to find someone who will do your analyses for you. Don't be daunted at this point. While the statistical techniques that are needed require someone who is statistically sophisticated, as can be seen above, the results of these analyses can be presented in a straightforward, understandable format.

If you are having a consultant do this work for you, you should ask for a report at this point that details the results of the focus groups and the phone survey. Further, based upon these results, request that the report detail promising social marketing approaches.

SOME CLOSING THOUGHTS

Identifying barriers is an essential first step in designing a successful program. While significant pressures exist to skip this step, the simple truth is that it is impossible to design an effective strategy without identifying barriers. In our experience, the four most common reasons for skipping barrier identification include:

♦ the belief that the barriers to the activity are already known,
♦ time pressures,
♦ financial constraints, and
♦ managerial staff who do not support conducting preliminary research.

Believing that the barriers to an activity are already known is very difficult to guard against. By our very nature we develop theories about why people behave as they do. If we didn't, we would find it difficult to understand and interact with others. This tendency to develop theories about the behavior of others can lead to a strong sense of assurance that the barriers to an activity are already well understood. Research in social psychology convincingly demonstrates, however, that once we have developed a "hunch" we tend to pay attention to information that supports our view, and discount or disregard information that would contradict it. As a consequence, we can come to believe very strongly in our own personal theories even though they may have no factual basis. To be an effective community-based social marketer requires a healthy dose of skepticism about your own and others' personal theories.

Conducting preliminary research to identify barriers and benefits takes time. In a well organized project you can expect the identification of barriers to add four to six weeks to the development of a strategy. However, the length of time required to identify barriers and benefits pales when compared to the time and effort involved in having to design and deliver a new program if the first is unsuccessful. Similarly, while identifying barriers and benefits adds to the expense of delivering a program, there is a high return on investment given the much greater likelihood of delivering a successful program.

Building support among managerial staff will often involve dealing directly with the above three concerns. Time and cost concerns can often be dealt with by noting, as discussed above, that identifying barriers and benefits will usually save both time and money by lessening the likelihood of having to mount multiple campaigns. Managers, like everyone else, develop theories about behavior and are just as prone to believe that they already know the barriers and benefits for the activity you are to promote. There is a strong likelihood that they may ascribe to either the attitude-behavior or economic self-interest approaches discussed in the previous chapter since these perspectives are widely accepted. Finally, arrange, if possible, for managerial staff to read this book or attend a workshop on community-based social marketing. In Canada, where the first edition of this book has been widely read, and workshops on community-based social marketing have been attended by a large number of managers, community-based social marketing is increasingly being specified by management as the method by which programs must be delivered.

Once you have identified the barriers to the activity you wish to promote, you will want to consider what behavior change tools you can use to overcome these barriers. Chapters 3 through 8 introduce a variety of tools that you can incorporate into the programs you design.

3

Commitment
From Good Intentions to Action

Our deeds determine us as much as
we determine our deeds
— George Elliot

Imagine being approached and asked to have a large, ugly, obtrusive billboard with the wording "DRIVE CAREFULLY" placed on your front lawn. When a researcher, posing as a volunteer, made precisely this request, numerous residents in a Californian neighborhood flatly declined.[1] That they declined is hardly surprising, especially since they were shown a picture of the billboard almost completely obscuring the view of another house. What is surprising, however, is that fully 76% of another group of residents in this study agreed to have the sign placed on their lawn. Why would over three-fourths of one group agree, while virtually everyone in the other group sensibly declined? The answer lies in something that happened to the second group prior to this outlandish request being made. The residents who agreed in droves to have this aberration placed on their lawn were previously asked if they would display in the windows of their cars or homes a small, three inch sign that said: "BE A SAFE DRIVER." This request was so innocuous that virtually everyone agreed to it. Agreeing to this trivial request, however, greatly increased the likelihood that they would subsequently consent to having the billboard placed on their lawn.

Are these findings a mere anomaly? Apparently not. In another study a researcher, identifying himself as a member of a consumer group, called and asked householders if he could ask them a few questions about their soap preferences.[2] A few days later the same researcher called back asking for a much larger favor: "Could I send five or six people through your house to obtain an inventory of all the products in the house?"The caller carefully explained that this "inventory" would require searching through all of their drawers, closets, etc. Having agreed to the smaller request only a few days earlier, many of the householders apparently felt compelled to agree with this much larger and more invasive request. Indeed, over 50% agreed, more than twice as many as among householders who had not received the prior request.

These surprising findings have now been replicated in a variety of settings. In each case, individuals who agreed to a small initial request were far more likely to agree to a subsequent larger request. For example:

♦ When asked if they would financially support a recreational facility for the handicapped, 92% made a donation if they had previously signed a petition in favor of the facility, compared with 53% for those who had not been asked to sign the petition.[3]

♦ Residents of Bloomington, Indiana, were called and asked if they would consider, hypothetically, spending three hours working as a volunteer collecting money for the American Cancer Society. When these individuals were called back three days later by a different individual, they were far more likely to volunteer than another group of residents who had not been asked the initial question (31% versus 4%, respectively).[4]

♦ A sample of registered voters were approached one day prior to a U.S. presidential election and asked:"Do you expect you will vote or not?" All agreed that they would vote. Relative to voters who were not asked this simple question, their likelihood of voting increased by 41%.[5]

♦ Ending a blood-drive telephone call with the query:"We'll count on seeing you then, OK?" increased the likelihood of individuals showing up from 62% to 81%.[6]

♦ Individuals who were asked to wear a lapel pin publicizing the Canadian Cancer Society were nearly twice as likely to

donate subsequently than were those who were not asked to
wear the pin.[7]

UNDERSTANDING COMMITMENT

Why does agreeing to a small request lead people to agree subsequently to a much larger one? When individuals agree to a small
request, it often alters the way they perceive themselves. That is,
when individuals sign a petition favoring the building of a new

*People have a strong
desire to be seen as
consistent by others*

facility for the handicapped, the act of signing subtly alters their
attitudes on the topic. In short, they come to view themselves as
the type of person who supports initiatives for the handicapped.
When asked later to comply with the larger request, giving a donation, there is strong internal pressure to behave "consistently."
Similarly, saying that you "think" you would volunteer for the
Cancer Society, vote in an election, give blood or wear a lapel pin,
alters your attitudes and increases the likelihood that you will later
act in a way that is consistent with your new attitudes.

Consistency is an important character trait.[8] Those who behave
inconsistently are often perceived as untrustworthy and unreliable. In contrast, individuals whose deeds match their words are
viewed as being honest and having integrity. The need in all of us
to behave consistently is underscored by an intriguing study on a
New York City beach. In this study, a researcher posing as a sunbather put a blanket down some five feet from a randomly select-

ed sunbather. He then proceeded to relax on the blanket for a few minutes while listening to his radio. When he got up he said to the person beside him, "Excuse me, I'm here alone and have no matches… do you have a light?" He then went for a walk on the beach, leaving the blanket and radio behind. Shortly afterward, another researcher, posing as a thief, stole the radio and fled down the beach. Under these circumstances, the thief was pursued 4 times out of 20 stagings. However, the results were dramatically different when the researcher made a modest request prior to taking the walk. When he asked the person beside him to "watch his things," in 19 out of the 20 stagings the individual leapt up to pursue the thief. When they caught him some restrained him, others grabbed the radio back, while others demanded an explanation. Almost all acted consistently with what they had said they would do.[9]

The need to behave consistently is further supported by findings that a substantial amount of time can pass between the first and second request, and that the second request can be made by a different individual. That considerable time can pass between the two requests provides further evidence that complying with the initial request alters the way we see ourselves in an enduring way. That we will comply with a second request initiated by a new person suggests that these changes are not transitory; otherwise we would only feel bound to comply if the second request were made by the same person who had made the initial request.

COMMITMENT AND SUSTAINABLE BEHAVIOR

As detailed above, commitment techniques have been shown to be effective in promoting a diverse variety of behaviors. This community-based social marketing tool has also been shown to be effective in promoting sustainable behavior. Here are several examples (citations for additional studies can be found at www.sustainable.stthomasu.ca):

♦ In research carried out with Pacific Gas and Electric, home assessors were trained to make use of commitment strategies as well as other community-based social marketing techniques.[10] The assessors were trained to secure a verbal commitment from the householder. For example, the householder might be asked:"When do you think that you'll have the weather-stripping completed?… I'll give you a call around then, just to see how it's coming along, and to see if you're having any problems."These subtle changes in how the assessment was presented resulted in substantial increases in the likelihood that householders would retrofit their homes. In fact, using community-based social marketing methods resulted in three to four times as many people electing to retrofit their homes.

When commitment was used along with other community based social marketing tools, 3 to 4 times as many people elected to retrofit their homes.

♦ Commitment techniques have also been applied in the retail sector. In this study, small retail firms were randomly assigned to either a "mild commitment,""strong commitment" or "control" condition.[11] In the "mild commitment" condition the names of the firms were published every other month along with information about the energy conservation initiative. In the "strong commitment" condition not only the names of the firms were published, but also the extent to which they had (or had not) saved energy. In all three cases, companies received information on steps they could take to reduce energy use and received a free energy audit. While the three groups did not differ in the amount of electricity they consumed, the two commitment conditions used significantly less natural gas than did the control group. Importantly, firms in the "mild commitment" condition used less natural gas than firms in the "strong commitment" condition. Informal comments from the owners of the companies in the "strong commitment" condition suggest that they felt trapped by the public disclosure of their initial lack of success in saving energy and that they subsequently stopped attempting to save energy. It is important to note that in this study there was no explicit commitment pledge. The researchers assumed that having their names publicly displayed would enhance commitment, but they did not directly ask for a commitment.

♦ Commitment has also been used to promote bus ridership. Individuals who did not ride the bus were assigned to one of four conditions. In the "information only" condition, participants received route and schedule information and an identification card that allowed ridership to be monitored. In the "commitment condition," participants made a verbal pledge to ride the bus twice a week for four weeks, while in the "incentive condition," participants were given ten free bus tickets and were informed that they could receive more tickets when they had used the initial tickets. Finally, in the "combined condition," participants both made a pledge to ride twice a week for four weeks and received free tickets. Each of the three conditions increased bus ridership. However, participants in the "commitment only" condition rode the bus just as frequently as the participants in the "incentive condition" and the "combined condition". Importantly, these effects were observable during two follow-ups, conducted at three and twelve weeks after the intervention.

*Written commitments
are more effective
than verbal commitments*

♦ In a unique study, homeowners were mailed either a shower flow restrictor along with a pamphlet on energy conservation or just the pamphlet alone.[12] Homes that received the shower flow restrictor in addition to the pamphlet were not only more likely to install the restrictor, an obvious finding, but were also more likely to engage in the other conservation actions mentioned in the pamphlet (e.g., lowering the temperature on their hot water heaters, installing setback thermostats and cleaning their furnaces). Apparently having installed the shower flow restrictor altered how these individuals perceived themselves. In short, they came to see themselves as the type of person who is concerned about energy conservation and, as a result, carried through with the other actions suggested in the pamphlet.

♦ Obtaining a signed commitment increased curbside recycling in Salt Lake City, Utah, more than receiving a flyer, a telephone call or personal contact alone.[13]

BUILDING COMMITMENT INTO YOUR PROGRAM

A variety of studies have clarified when the community-based social marketing tool, commitment, is likely to be most effective. Written commitments appear to be more effective than verbal commitments.[14] In a study that investigated the impact of verbal versus written commitments, households were assigned to one of three groups. In the first group, homes simply received a pamphlet underscoring the importance of recycling newspaper. In the second group, households made a verbal pledge to recycle newsprint, while in the third group, households signed a statement in which they committed themselves to recycle newsprint. Initially, the households who made either a verbal or written commitment recycled more newsprint than households who received only a pamphlet. However, only the households who committed themselves by signing the statement were still recycling when a follow-up was conducted.

Percent Reduction in Electricty and Natural Gas

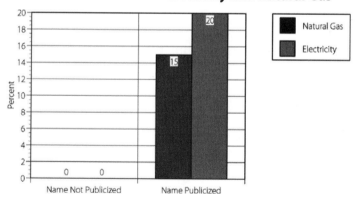

Whenever possible, ask permission to make a commitment public. The dramatic impact that public commitments can have is illustrated in a study in which either a private commitment to conserve electricity and natural gas was obtained or a public commitment in which names would be published in the local newspaper. Those who agreed to a public commitment saved significantly more energy than did householders who were in the private condition. Even after the researchers informed the participants who had agreed to a public commitment that their names would not be published, they continued to save energy. While the names were never publicized, simply asking for this permission brought about a 15% reduction in natural gas used and a 20% reduction in electricity used. Importantly, these reductions were still observable 12 months later.[15] Public commitments are likely so effective because of our desire to be consistent. In short, the more public a commitment, the more likely we are to honor it.

Seeking commitments in groups can also be effective. When the economic and environmental benefits of recycling were explained to members of a retirement home, and they were asked to make a group commitment, there was a 47% increase in the amount of paper recycled.[16] The authors suggest that group commitments are likely to be effective in settings where there is good group cohesion. This suggests group commitments are likely to be effective in well established groups in which individuals care how they are viewed by other members of the group.

Commitment can be increased not only by seeking a verbal or written pledge, but also through actively involving the person. In the Pacific Gas and Electric study mentioned above, home assessors were trained to involve the homeowner actively in the assessment.[17] Homeowners were asked to peer into the attic to inspect the insulation level, to place their hand on an uninsulated water heater, etc. After being involved in this way, homeowners are more likely to see themselves as committed to energy conservation.

Commitment strategies have been criticized as too labor intensive to warrant implementing on a broad scale.[18] However, implementing commitment as part of a home visit, as was done in the

Pacific Gas and Electric study, is a viable option. Further, asking for a commitment when a service is provided, such as delivery of a compost unit or a water efficiency kit, is a natural opportunity to employ this strategy. Two other strategies are worth considering in making use of commitment. First, existing volunteer groups can be used. In one study, Boy Scouts asked residents to sign a statement agreeing to participate in a community recycling program. Those households who were asked to sign the statement were much more likely to participate than was a control group who was not asked (42% and 11%, respectively).[19]

Commitments made by cohesive groups can be very effective

Commitment strategies have also been shown to be effective when community "block leaders" implement them. A block leader is a community resident who already engages in the behavior that is being promoted and agrees to speak to other people in their immediate community to help them get started. In this study, block leaders approached homes and used a variety of communi-ty-based social marketing strategies, including seeking a verbal commitment, to encourage the household to begin recycling. The homes who were visited by a block leader were more than twice as likely to recycle as was a group who received flyers.[20]

Commitment can also be made cost-effective by asking people who commit to trying a new behavior to ask others to make a similar commitment. In an important study, residents who had been previously identified as putting their grass clippings at the curbside for disposal, were assigned into three groups. The first group was approached and asked to make a commitment to leave their clippings on their lawn, while the second was asked to make a commitment to grass cycle and to ask their neighbors to do the same. The "commitment only" request had no effect on grass cycling. However, those who were asked to speak to their neighbors, as well as make a personal commitment to grass cycle, increased not only their own grass cycling but also that of their neighbors. Importantly, these findings were still observable twelve months later.

Commitments should be sought only for behaviors which people express interest in doing. Hence, if a block leader approaches a home and asks if the residents are interested in composting, commitment should only be sought if the household expresses an interest in the activity. Indeed, research suggests that commitment will not work if the person feels pressured to commit. In order for commitment to be effective, the commitment must be voluntary.

Earlier in this chapter we suggested that one of the reasons for the dramatic impact of small requests upon subsequent behavior was that responding to a small request alters how we see ourselves. If how we see ourselves is an important predictor of how we will act in the future, it makes sense that programs to promote sustainable behavior should actively assist people to see themselves as environmentally concerned. Support for this assertion comes from a study that investigated the impact of assisting people to see themselves as charitable.[21] In this study, householders were approached and asked if they would make a donation to the heart association. Half of the individuals who volunteered to make a donation were thanked and told, "You are a generous person. I wish more of the people I met were as charitable as you," while the other half were simply thanked. One to two weeks later these same individuals were approached by another individual and asked if they would donate money to Multiple Sclerosis. Not only did more of the "generously labeled" people give money to Multiple Sclerosis, they also gave more — fully 75% more. This research suggests that when possible we should be helping people to see themselves as environmentally concerned. For example, when encouraging someone to try a new activity, such as composting, we should begin by pointing out the other positive sustainable behaviors that they are already involved in.

When people make a commitment, request that they ask others to make a similar commitment

Finally, commitment is most effective when combined with other community-based social marketing tools. In particular, whenever community-based social marketing tools are utilized they should be combined with the principles of effective communication discussed in Chapter 6. For example, in a project to increase recycling in an apartment complex, residents were randomly assigned to one of four groups: feedback only, public commitment only, feedback and commitment combined, or a control group.[22] Residents in the feedback and public commitment groups did not increase the amount of paper they recycled. However, residents in the "feedback" and "feedback and public commitment" groups significantly increased the amount of paper they recycled (26% and 40%, respectively).

A CHECKLIST FOR USING COMMITMENT

In considering using commitment, check that the following guidelines have been followed:

♦ Emphasize written over verbal commitments
♦ Ask for public commitments
♦ Seek groups' commitments
♦ Actively involve the person
♦ Consider cost-effective ways to obtain commitments
♦ Use existing points of contact to obtain commitments
♦ Help people to view themselves as environmentally concerned
♦ Don't use coercion (commitments must be freely volunteered)
♦ Combine commitment with other behavior change techniques

Most of the research that has investigated the use of commitment techniques has occurred in the areas of energy and water efficiency and waste reduction. While commitment research has been primarily limited to these three areas, it is possible to use commitment strategies to promote a variety of different forms of sustainable behavior. The accompanying box contains a variety of examples of how commitments can be used to foster sustainable behavior. In conclusion, obtaining a commitment is a powerful way of increasing public participation rates in sustainable behavior. When combined with other community-based social marketing strategies, commitment further enhances the likelihood that your community-based social marketing strategy will be effective. In the next chapter, we will see how prompts can be used to remind people to engage in sustainable behavior.

EXAMPLES: USING COMMITMENT TO FOSTER SUSTAINABLE BEHAVIOR

WASTE REDUCTION

♦ When distributing compost units, ask when the person expects to begin to use the unit and inquire if you can call shortly afterward to see if he/she is having any difficulties.

♦ Ask households who have just been delivered a compost unit to place a sticker on the side of their recycling container indicating that they compost.

♦ Ask people as they enter grocery stores to wear a button or sticker supporting the purchase of products that have recycled content or are recyclable (see also Chapter 5 on norm development).

♦ In retail outlets, place decals on household hazardous waste containers that provide information on where HHW can be taken for proper disposal. Partner with retail outlets to have customers sign the decal commiting themselves to taking unused amounts of the product to the depot for proper disposal.

ENERGY CONSERVATION

♦ As mentioned previously in this chapter, when conducting a home assessment, invite the homeowners to participate.

♦ Conclude a home assessment visit by asking when they expect to complete activities such as weather-stripping or installing a programmable thermostat. Call back to help homeowners troubleshoot any problems they had with installation.

WATER CONSERVATION

♦ Ask households to sign a pledge form committing themselves to watering their lawn on odd or even days based on their house number.

... more ...

- Ask homeowners to make a commitment to raise the height of their lawnmower, thereby reducing evaporation and the need for lawn watering.
- In going door-to-door with water efficiency kits (toilet dams, faucet aerators and low-flow shower heads), ask homeowners who wish to take the kit to make a public commitment to install it (e.g., have their names advertised in the newspaper).

Transportation

- Ask commuters to sign a public commitment that they will take mass transit once or twice a week for a specific period of time (see the study on bus ridership in this chapter).
- Ask car owners to commit to turn their car off while waiting to pick someone up. Provide a prompt that they can affix to their windshield or dashboard to remind them to turn their engine off (see the next chapter on prompts).
- Ask car owners to commit publicly to checking their car tire pressure once a month. Provide prompts at gas stations reminding people to check their tire pressure. Have gas attendants also commit to reminding people to check their tire pressure.

For examples of *committment* cases and graphics visit www.cbsm.com

Prompts
Remembering to Act Sustainably

4

Consistency is contrary to nature, contrary to life
The only completely consisten people are the dead
— *Aldous Huxley*

Many people have bought cotton shopping bags to use in place of the plastic bags stores provide. While we expect that the people who have bought these bags prefer to use them whenever they shop, we also expect that like ourselves, they frequently leave them behind in the house or car. The problem is not a lack of motivation to use the bags, but rather simply forgetting to bring them.

Numerous actions that promote sustainability are susceptible to the most human of traits: forgetting. Turning off lights upon leaving a room, turning down the thermostat in the evening, checking the air pressure in our tires and selecting products that have recycled-content while shopping are just a few of the many actions that we are apt to forget to do. In some cases, innovations such as a programmable thermostat can free us from the burden of continually remembering to carry out an activity. Most repetitive actions, however, have no simple "technological fix."

Fortunately, "prompts" are effective in reminding people to engage in sustainable behaviors. A prompt is a visual or auditory aid which reminds us to carry out an activity that we might otherwise forget. The purpose of a prompt is not to change attitudes or increase motivation, but simply to remind us to engage in an action that we are already predisposed to do.

PROMPTS AND SUSTAINABLE BEHAVIOR

Prompts abound. Slogans, such as "Act Locally, Think Globally," "Keep California Beautiful," and "Don't Be Fuelish," are all designed to promote sustainable behaviors. Despite a prevalent belief that prompts such as these are effective in promoting sustainable behavior, nonexplicit prompts ordinarily have little or no impact.[1]

Prompts that target specific behaviors can, however, have a substantial impact. Here are several examples:

♦ Scott Geller and his colleagues demonstrated the effectiveness of prompts in promoting the purchase of returnable soft drink bottles.[2] At two supermarkets and one convenience store the percentage of returnable bottles normally purchased was determined. After obtaining this baseline data, they distributed flyers at each of the three stores requesting that shoppers purchase soft drinks in returnable bottles. At the two supermarkets the prompts had no impact upon the purchase of returnable bottles. At the convenience store, however, the flyers increased the purchase of returnable bottles by 32%! Why were the flyers effective in the convenience store but not the supermarkets? For prompts to be effective they need to be delivered near the desired behavior. In the large supermarkets, where shoppers are buying many items, the delivery of the flyers likely occurred well before the purchase of soft drinks. In contrast, in the convenience store, where only a few items are conventionally purchased, the delay between the presentation of the flyer and the purchase of soft drinks was much shorter.

♦ Jeffrey Smith and Russell Bennett have shown that prompts can be very effective in discouraging people from walking across lawns.[3] At four separate locations 79% of pedestrians were found to cut across a lawn rather than taking a slightly longer pathway. However, when a sign with the message, "Do not cut across the grass," was placed at these four sites, lawn-walking decreased by 46%. Lawn-walking was reduced even further when a second sign was added that said "Cutting across the grass will save 10 seconds." Indeed, when these two signs were present, lawn-walking was reduced to only 8%.

♦ Litter receptacles serve as a visual prompt for the proper disposal of garbage. Simply making a litter receptacle more visually interesting was found to double the amount of litter deposited in one study and increase it by 61% in another.[4,5]

Prompts can be very effective in encouraging repetitive behaviors, such as closing blinds

♦ Retrofitting older buildings is the most effective way to reduce their energy use, but for many organizations the cost of a retrofit is prohibitively expensive.[6] Simple lifestyle changes can, however, have a significant impact upon energy use, often with no capital expense. One such example involved encouraging university faculty to drop and tilt their blinds when they left their offices at the end of the day to reduce heat loss during the winter. Baseline data was collected by cleaning staff who recorded whether blinds were dropped and tilted correctly (concave surface of the blind tilted into the room to deflect heat back into the room). Faculty were encouraged to drop-and-tilt their blinds through a general written request from the university president and by having the cleaning staff leave a reminder on the desk of faculty who forgot to drop-and-tilt their blinds. These two simple methods increased the percentage of faculty who adjusted their blinds from less than 10% to roughly two-thirds.

◆ Compared to baseline, the introduction of more conveniently located recycling containers and the use of prompts increased the amount of newspaper recycled in three apartment complexes from 50 to 100%.[7]

◆ Following the introduction of verbal and visual prompts in a high school cafateria, littering was reduced by over 350%.[8]

◆ Prompts have also been shown to have a substantial impact upon paper recycling.[9] In one department at Florida State University, a prompt that read "Recyclable Materials" was placed directly above a recycling container. The prompt indicated the types of paper to be recycled, while another prompt over the trash receptacle read "No Paper Products." The addition of these two simple prompts increased the percentage of fine paper captured by 54%, while in another department the same procedure increased the capture rate by 29%.

These and other studies support the notion that to be effective, a prompt should be delivered as close in space and time as possible to the target behavior. Accordingly, place prompts to turn off lights on or beside the light switch by the exit. Similarly, prompts to purchase products that contain recycled content should be on the store shelf at the point of sale.

PROMPTS AND SOURCE REDUCTION

Several initiatives to encourage source reduction are demonstrating just how effective prompts can be in promoting sustainable behavior.

The Minnesota Office of Waste Management has designed a program entitled SMART (Saving Money And Reducing Trash) that provides communities with various educational materials for shoppers. One element of this program is the "shelf talker." Shelf talkers are prompts that identify products that reduce waste and save money. Similarly, the Champaign, Illinois, Central States Education Center uses posters, flyers and shelf labels to indicate products that are environmentally friendly.[10] This program identifies items that either are recyclable locally, have less packaging, or are "safer-earth" products (e.g., non-toxic cleaners). Affixing 700 long-term labels throughout a store takes several hours, considerably less time than it takes to adjust the 17,000 price labels that, on average, are changed weekly. Analysis of supermarket store inventory suggests that the use of these prompts has shifted purchases to recyclable containers. The impact upon the purchase of "least-waste packages" and "safer earth products" has not yet been determined.[11]

In Seattle, Washington, a "Get in the Loop, Buy Recycled" campaign has been operating for several years.[12] Like the other initiatives, this program utilizes "shelftalkers" that identify products with recycled content. The program is advertised through television, radio and newspaper advertisements by both the King County Commission for Marketing Recyclable Materials and participating retailers. In 1994, 850 retailers in western Washington state participated. Relative to the month preceding the launch of the 1994 campaign, sales of recycled-content products increased nearly 30%.[13] Sales of specific product categories have shown even more dramatic increases. For example, sales of recycled-content paper products have increased by 74%.

BUILDING PROMPTS INTO YOUR PROGRAM

Prompts can be effective for encouraging both one-time and repetitive behaviors that promote sustainability. One-time behaviors, as the name suggests, refer to actions that individuals engage in only once, but that result in an ongoing positive environmental impact (e.g., installing a clock thermostat, connecting a low-flow showerhead). Because these behaviors have to be engaged in only once, they are often easier to influence than repetitive behaviors, where an individual has to engage in an action repeatedly for there to be a significant environmental benefit (e.g., composting, source reduction). Given the difficulty of making lifestyle changes that promote sustainability, prompts may be of particular use in establishing and maintaining repetitive behaviors that favor sustainability.

Providing a prompt at the point-of-sale can dramatically increase the purchase of environmentally friendly products

A CHECKLIST FOR USING PROMPTS

In considering using prompts, follow these guidelines.

♦ Make the prompt noticeable.

♦ The prompt should be self-explanatory. Through graphics and/or text the prompt should explain simply what the person is to do (e.g., turn off the lights).

♦ The prompt should be presented as close in time and space as possible to the targeted behavior (e.g., place a prompt to turn off lights directly on a light switch; place a prompt to purchase a product with recycled content directly below the product).

♦ Use prompts to encourage people to engage in positive behaviors rather than to avoid environmentally harmful actions (e.g., use prompts to encourage people to buy environmentally friendly products rather than to dissuade them from purchasing environmentally harmful products).

♦ Use commitment strategies (see the previous chapter) and norms (see the following chapter) to encourage people to act on the prompt.

Below are several examples of how prompts can be used to foster sustainable behavior.

EXAMPLES: USING PROMPTS TO FOSTER SUSTAINABLE BEHAVIOR

WASTE REDUCTION

♦ Use "shelf talkers" at the point-of-sale to promote source reduction.

Affix decals to paint cans providing information on where to dispose of left-over paint

♦ Distribute grocery list pads that remind shoppers every time they look at their grocery list to shop for products that have recycled content, are recylable, or have least-waste packaging.

♦ Place signs at the entrances to supermarkets reminding shoppers to bring their reusable shopping bags into the store. Also, distribute car window stickers with the purchase of reusable shopping bags; the stickers can be put on the window next to the car lock to remind people to bring their reusable bags into the store.

... more ...

- Have check-out clerks ask consumers if they have brought bags with them.
- Affix decals to potentially hazardous household products during home assessments that indicate vividly (see Chapter 6) that the product must be disposed of properly. The decal should contain information on where to dispose of hazardous waste and a contact number.
- Attach a decal to the side of recycling containers indicating what can be recycled. When what can be recycled changes, simply place a new decal over the old one.
- Attach a decal to compost units indicating organics that can be composted and the basics of composting. Better yet, since neither what can be composted nor the basics of composting changes, require that this information be stamped directly onto the compost unit.

Energy Conservation

- Affix decals directly to light switches to prompt that lights be turned off when rooms are vacant.
- Affix removable decals to the dashboards of new cars prompting drivers to turn off their engines while parked.
- Use signs to encourage drivers to turn off their engines while parked in locations where drivers frequently wait (schools, train stations, loading docks, etc.).
- Affix decals to dishwashers and washing machines encouraging that they only be used when there is a full load.
- Affix decals to all appliances which indicate the relative energy efficiency of the appliance (e.g. indicate the second price tag). This is presently done for major appliances in Canada.

... more ...

WATER CONSERVATION

♦ To encourage lawn watering on odd or even days, ask each homeowner for permission to place a tag on the outside water faucet.

♦ Arrange with local retailers to attach decals to lawnmowers that encourage householders to raise the level of the lawnmower. Additionally, this decal can encourage that the grass clippings be left on the lawn (mulched) as a natural nutrient.

♦ Have homeowners place an empty tuna can in the garden (to measure adequate watering). When the can is filled with water the garden or lawn has been adequately watered.

Attach a prompt to outside faucets reminding home-owners to water their lawn on odd or even days

♦ Attach decals to dishwashers and washing machines in retail stores encouraging full loads.

♦ Attach decals to low-flow toilets and shower heads indicating that they save water and money.

... more ...

TRANSPORTATION

- ◆ Encourage motorists to turn off their engines while waiting to pick someone up by placing signs in common waiting areas (train stations, bus depots, school parking lots, etc.)
- ◆ Use prompts along with commitments to encourage car owners to have their car engines regularly tuned-up and their tires properly inflated.

For examples of *prompt* cases and graphics visit www.cbsm.com

Norms
Building Community Support

Belief, like any other moving body, follows
the path of least resistance.
— Samuel Butler

Imagine that you have agreed to participate in an experiment on visual discrimination. Upon arriving for the study, you are asked to take your place at a table at which five other participants are seated. As you take your seat, the experimenter explains that this study will involve making perceptual judgments regarding the lengths of four lines. He then projects an image on the screen at the front of the room. On the left side of the screen there is a line labelled "X." On the other side of the screen are three lines, labelled "A," "B" and "C." Your task, he explains, is a simple one: to

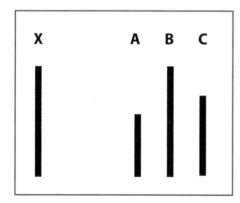

select which of lines "A," "B" or "C" is equivalent in length to line "X." The experimenter then proceeds to show a variety of slides. For each slide the other participants and you are asked to select the line that is equal to "X." After several slides, you are beginning to yawn and wonder how someone ever received a grant to conduct this research. On the next slide, however, something unexpected happens. In response to the set of lines above, the first participant selects line "C" as the line that is equal to "X." You rub your eyes and look again. Yes, she did say "C" — but clearly that is wrong, you think to yourself. Your train of thought is broken as the next participant also reports that line "C" is equal to "X." After the third, fourth, and fifth participants also select "C" you begin to question your own visual abilities, mentally make a note to have your eyes checked and then utter what a moment ago was unthinkable. "Line C," you hear yourself saying, "is the correct choice."

When Solomon Asch conducted this study, approximately 75% of the participants altered their answers at least once to concur with the incorrect answers of others in the group (who, as you have by now surmised, were accomplices of the experimenter).[1] Perhaps you are thinking that these visual discriminations were difficult enough to lead participants to really question their selections. Unfortunately, they were not. When participants were left on their own to select which of the three lines was the correct match, the correct line was selected 99% of the time.

Asch's research is both surprising and troubling. In response to the findings, Asch wrote: "That reasonably intelligent and well-meaning young people are willing to call white black is a matter of concern." Asch's findings are not unique, however. In a variety of settings, people have been found to alter their answers to be in line (no pun intended) with normative, though clearly incorrect, answers given by others.

What is fascinating about Asch's study, and other research on conformity, is that the tasks are often completely inconsequential. In the larger scheme of things, it simply doesn't matter which of the lines is equal to "X." Nonetheless, people looked to the behavior of those around them to determine how they would respond.

Asch's research underscores the important role that other people have upon our own behavior. To date, too little attention has been given to the significant impact that norms can have upon the adoption of sustainable behavior. If we are to make the transition to a sustainable future, it is critical that we are able to develop a new set of societal norms that support sustainable lifestyles. This chapter will introduce you to research which demonstrates the powerful influence that norms have upon behavior, and provide guidelines for integrating the use of norms into the programs you deliver.

SOCIAL NORMS AND SUSTAINABLE BEHAVIOR

During the 1930's, both American and Canadian farmers were losing dramatic amounts of topsoil from their fields. In response to this crisis, the U.S. government distributed brochures which detailed the problem and suggested actions, such as planting trees as wind screens, that could be taken to slow the loss of topsoil. Like the information campaigns discussed in Chapter 1, this attempt to influence the behavior of farmers was a dismal failure. When it was clear that farmers were not changing their agricultural practices, the government tried a new approach that involved working directly with a small number of farmers. These farmers received direct assistance in adopting practices that would slow erosion. It was reasoned that farmers might be more apt to adopt new approaches if these new approaches were first modelled by a farmer in their area. Modelling a new technique, such as installing wind screens or alternative methods of tillage, it was believed, would be far more compelling than dryly describing the technique in a pamphlet. Further, it would encourage local farmers to discuss the new technique and, if they observed that it was working successfully on a local farm, increase the likelihood that they would adopt it themselves. Unlike the information campaign, this approach was far more successful. Neighboring farmers observed the changes that these farmers were making, discussed them with them, and adopted similar practices once they saw the results. As a consequence, these new agricultural practices spread quickly.[2]

More recently, several studies have documented the impact that modelling and social norms can have upon individuals engaging in sustainable behavior. At the University of California, Santa Cruz, athletic complex, the male shower room had a sign that encouraged that the showers be turned off while users soap up.[3] More specifically, the sign read:"Conserve water: 1. Wet down. 2. Water off. 3. Soap. 4. Rinse." This sign apparently had little effect on behavior. On average, only 6% of users were found to comply. One possibility was that people simply didn't see the sign. However, a survey of a random sample of students demonstrated that 93% were aware of the sign and its message.

Elliot Aronson and Michael O'Leary reasoned that students might be far more likely to comply with the sign if they observed another student following its instructions. To test this possibility, an accomplice entered the male shower room in the athletic complex and proceeded to the back of the room and turned on the shower. When another student entered, the accomplice turned off the shower, soaped up and then turned on the shower once more to rinse off. All of this was done with his back to the other student and without eye contact. When the accomplice modelled water conservation in this way, the percentage of students who turned off the shower to soap up shot up to 49%. Further, when two accomplices modelled water conservation, the number of people who followed suit rose to 67%. It is important to note that the changes in behavior observed in this study were not brought about by punitive measures. No "shower police" intervened if students did not turn off the shower while soaping up (Note that two community-based social marketing strategies are employed in this study: prompts [the sign] and norms. While the sign by itself was ineffective in altering the behavior of those using the shower room, when it was combined with the norm, behavior changed dramatically. When possible, look for opportunities to use more

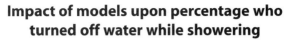

Impact of models upon percentage who turned off water while showering

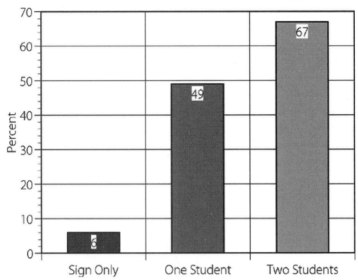

than one community-based social marketing tool at a time). As is further evidenced in the following study, in many situations it is sufficient to make a community norm salient by modelling it in order to have a substantial impact upon behavior.

Picture yourself leaving the local library and walking toward your car in the parking lot. As you get closer to your car, you notice that someone has left one of those annoying flyers under not only your windshield wipers, but everyone else's as well. You remove the flyer and crumple it up, but do you toss it on the ground? We are well aware that most of the people who are going to read this book will take the flyer home and put it in their recycling container, but what would "most other" people do in this situation? The answer, it turns out, depends upon what those around them do. In a series of ingenious studies, Robert Cialdini and his colleagues placed flyers on every windshield in a library parking lot.[4] In one condition, as library patrons made their way back to their cars an accomplice walked past, picked up a littered bag and placed it in a garbage can. In the control condition, the accomplice simply walked past and did nothing. What impact did these simple acts have upon the library patrons? For those who observed the littered bag being picked up and thrown in the garbage, virtually no one littered the flyer. However, when the accomplice simply walked past and left the bag on the ground, over one-third threw the flyer on the ground! In a related study, Cialdini and his colleagues removed the human model and simply manipulated the number of flyers that were strewn about in the parking lot. When the parking lot was littered with flyers, the library patrons littered as well. However, when only one flyer was littered in the parking lot, patrons littered significantly less.

Community norms may be the most effective way to discourage the use of pesticides and herbicides on lawns

USING NORMS EFFECTIVELY

Clearly, perceived norms can have a substantial impact upon behavior. How might they best be used to promote sustainable behavior? To answer this question, it is useful first to consider two distinct ways in which norms affect behavior: compliance and conformity. In compliance, individuals alter their behavior to receive a reward, to provoke a favourable reaction from others, or to avoid being punished. The change in behavior occurs not because the person believes that the behavior is "the right thing to do," but rather because there is a tangible consequence for not doing the behavior. Compliance tactics, such as bottle deposits or charging user fees for waste disposal, are effective as long as the rewards or punishments are in place (see Chapter 7). Once the rewards and punishments are removed, the gains made by using compliance tactics are often lost. While compliance techniques can have substantial impacts upon behavior, often they are not cost-effective to administer. In contrast, conformity that occurs due to individuals observing the behavior of others in order to determine how they should behave can have long-lasting effects.

Where possible, then, programs to promote sustainable behavior should attempt to communicate what are accepted behaviors. For example, communicating that the vast majority of people living in a community strongly believe that it is important to reduce waste, and that they demonstrate this belief through participating in curbside recycling programs, can be an effective way to bolster recycling as well as to introduce other waste reduction programs such as composting and source reduction. By stressing the very high participation rates in blue box recycling, clear messages are sent to others regarding the perceived importance of waste reduction

To be effective, the norm must also be visible. Certain sustainable behaviors, such as composting, are almost invisible in a community. Unlike blue box recycling, which demonstrates a community norm every time people put their containers at the curbside, composting happens in the backyard, out of view. How can composting be made more visible? Attaching stickers that proclaim "This Household Composts" to the side of the recycling or garbage container can help to create and maintain a community norm for composting each time these containers are taken to the curbside.

Households who were visited by a block leader were more likely to report that they felt upset if they discarded recyclable materials and that they felt an obligation to recycle these materials.

For norms to be effective they need to be internalized by people. That is, people need to view the behavior which the norm prescribes as the way they "should" behave. Several studies demonstrate that it is possible to influence the acceptance of such norms. Joseph Hopper and Joyce McCarl Nielsen believe that an important motivation to recycle is the belief that it is simply the " right thing to do" (a norm), despite the fact that it takes time and can be inconvenient. Further, they expect that this norm is most likely to develop through direct contact between people rather than through campaigns that rely upon prompts or information alone. To test these assumptions, the authors arranged for a sample of homes in Colorado to be divided into three groups.[5] In one group, households were visited by a volunteer block leader who spoke with them about curbside recycling, encouraged them to recycle, and then provided a prompt (reminder notice) several days before the monthly recycling collection date. In contrast, in the prompt group, households received a reminder notice a few days before the collection day, while in the information group households received a flyer that described the recycling program, indicated what items were acceptable and provided the collection dates. Those households who were visited by a volunteer block leader recycled nearly a third more often than households who received prompts and nearly three times as often as the homes who received the information flyer (further evidence of the ineffectiveness of information-based campaigns in bringing about behavior change). Not only were the volunteer block leaders most effective in altering behavior, but they alone had an impact upon norms. In comparing survey results from before and after this campaign, households who were visited by a block leader were more likely to report that they felt upset if they discarded recyclable materials and that they felt an obligation to recycle these materials. The prompt and information strategies had no impact upon these beliefs. For example, many anti-littering campaigns have as their central message that littering is simply not acceptable behavior. When Oklahoma City initiated an anti-littering campaign in 1987, community norms regarding littering changed substantially. Prior to the campaign, 37% of the community indicated they would feel guilty if they littered. Two years following the campaign that figure had risen to 67%. The number of people who believed they would lose the respect of others if they littered nearly tripled in the same time period.[6]

Finally, normative strategies are likely to be particularly effective when people are being asked to change their behavior or adopt a different lifestyle. In these cases, behavioral research suggests that direct contact in which social norms, modelling (see Chapter 6), and social diffusion (see Chapter 6) occur may be particularly important.[7]

A CHECKLIST FOR USING NORMS

Follow these guidelines in using norms:

♦ The norm should be noticeable.

♦ As with prompts, the norm should be made explicit at the time the targeted behavior is to occur (e.g., Upon entering a supermarket, customers could be greeted by a prominent display that indicates the percentage of shoppers who purposely select products that favor the environment).

♦ As with prompts, when possible use norms to encourage people to engage in positive behaviors rather than to avoid environmentally harmful actions.

Below are a variety of suggestions for using norms to promote sustainable behavior.

EXAMPLES: USING NORMS TO FOSTER SUSTAINABLE BEHAVIOR

WASTE REDUCTION

♦ Affix a decal to the recycling container indicating that "We Compost."

♦ Affix a decal to the recycling container indicating that the household buys recycled products.

♦ Ask supermarket shoppers to wear a button or sticker which shows their support for buying products that are recyclable or have recycled content (note that agreeing to wear a button or sticker also increases the likelihood that they will *actually* shop for these products — see Chapter 3).

... more ...

ENERGY CONSERVATION

♦ Attach gas mileage bumper stickers to very fuel- efficient cars.

♦ Attach to energy-efficient products in stores decals which indicate the number of people who believe it is important to purchase products that are more environmentally friendly.

WATER CONSERVATION

♦ Communicate the percentage of people who comply with municipal requests to restrict summer water use.

TRANSPORTATION

♦ Communicate the number of people in an organization who use mass transit, car pooling, walking or bicycling to get to work.

For examples of *norm* cases and graphics visit www.cbsm.com

6

Communication
Creating Effective Messages

My opinion, my conviction, gains infinitely in strength and success, the moment a second mind has adopted it.

— *Novalis*

The morning that I (Doug) began to write this chapter, my four year-old daughter and I had breakfast together. Taryn often uses breakfast as a time to plan what we will do together when I return from work. At four, Taryn has already mastered many of the finer points of persuasion. She understands that to persuade me she must first secure my attention. Further, she realizes that she must compete with her sister, my wife, the radio, the morning newspaper and my own preoccupations, if she is going to obtain a commitment to do one of her favorite things when I return from work.

Taryn usually secures my attention by asking that I sit with her at the children's table in our kitchen. This table has only two chairs, is secluded in a corner and, given its small size, places us very close together. Further, the table is too small an area upon which to open the morning paper. From Taryn's perspective, the setting is perfect.

Once I am sitting at the table and she has my full attention, the real persuasion occurs. In the summer, my daughter has three activities that she prefers above all others: going for a hike at a nearby beaver pond, having a picnic and swim at the wading pool, or going to the playground down the street (which just happens to be very close to the best place to get ice cream in Fredericton).

Taryn rarely begins by suggesting all three options. Instead, she begins with the most preferred and least likely, going to the beaver pond. She understands that we will only go to the beaver pond once or twice a week, so on any particular day she has little chance of persuading me to go there with her. Nonetheless, she always starts with the beaver pond. When I begin to explain why we can't go to the beaver pond (we were there yesterday), she cuts me off by saying: "I've got a deal for you. We won't go to the beaver pond, but we can go to the wading pool and have a picnic." On that particular evening, we have a friend coming for dinner and so the picnic is ruled out. Finally, Taryn strategically turns to her third option: going to the playground down the street. Unconsciously she understands that she has the upper hand as she has already conceded the beaver pond and the wading pool. As a skilled negotiator, she knows that it is my turn to make a concession. Once she realizes that I am beginning to say yes, she closes the deal by suggesting that after the playground we can get some of the ice cream that I like (she makes no mention of her having any). As soon as I agree, she immediately says: "It's a deal, then?" As I acknowledge that "it's a deal," she gets up from the table to tell her sister that we are going to the playground after supper (making my commitment public), and then for ice cream, while I am left to ponder how once again I have been out maneuvered by a four year-old who is only going to become more skilled with age.

Much of human communication involves persuasion. Whether done by a four year-old or a marketing firm, the aims are the same: to influence our attitudes and/or our behavior. The transition to a sustainable future will require that the vast majority of people be persuaded to adopt different lifestyles. How can we most effectively persuade people to adopt lifestyles supportive of sustainability? The purpose of this chapter is to outline some of the critical aspects of effective persuasion.

USE CAPTIVATING INFORMATION

All persuasion begins with capturing attention. Without attention, persuasion is impossible. In a review of pamphlets and flyers produced by governmental agencies and utilities on energy conservation, Paul Stern and Elliot Aronson found that most of the reviewed materials did not meet this most basic requirement.[1] The material reviewed was inconspicuous, boring or both.

How do we capture the attention of those we wish to persuade? While ideally we would like to sit them down at a very small corner table, where we know we have their undivided attention, we have to resort to other means. One of the most effective ways to ensure attention is to present information that is vivid, concrete and personalized.

All persuasion begins with capturing attention. Without attention, persuasion is impossible.

There are a variety of ways in which information can be made vivid, concrete and personal. For example, in a home energy audit a home assessor might utilize the householder's utility bills in describing money that is being lost by not retrofitting. Further, the assessor can provide information about similar people who have installed resource-conserving devices or describe "super-conservers" who have been exceptionally effective in reducing resource consumption.[2]

The power of vividly presented information has been demonstrated in a unique experiment carried out in California.[3] Marti Hope Gonzales and her colleagues trained nine of Pacific Gas and Electric's home assessors to present information in a manner that was psychologically compelling (they were also trained to seek a commitment; see Chapter 3). Normally, assessors provide feedback to the householder regarding energy efficiency by noting the absence of insulation in a basement or attic, cracks around windows or doors, etc. However, in this study the assessors were trained to present this same information vividly. Below is an example of what the assessors were trained to say:

> You know, if you were to add up all the cracks around and under these doors here, you'd have the equivalent of a hole the size of a football in your living room wall. Think for a moment about all the heat that would escape from a hole that size. That's why I recommend you install weatherstripping … And your attic totally lacks insulation. We professionals call that a naked attic. It's as if your home is facing winter not just without an overcoat, but without any clothing at all. (p. 1052)

Writing on the importance of presenting information vividly in home assessments, the authors state:

> Psychologically, a crack is seen as minor, but a hole the size of a football feels disastrous. The fact that they encompass the same area is of interest to an engineer; but in the mind of the average homeowner, the football will loom larger than the cracks under the door. Similarly, insulation is something with which most people lack experience, but the idea of a naked attic in the winter is something that forces attention and increases the probability of action (p. 1052).

Similarly, in describing the amount of waste produced annually by Californians, Shawn Burn at the California Polytechnic State University depicts the waste as "enough to fill a two-lane highway, ten feet deep from Oregon to the Mexican border."[4] Clearly, her depiction is much more vivid than simply saying that Californians each produce 1,300 lbs. of waste annually.

Why is vivid information effective? Vivid information increases the likelihood that a message will be attended to initially, a process called encoding, as well as recalled later. That is, information that is vivid is likely to stand out against all the other information that is competing for our attention. Further, because it is vivid, we are more likely to remember the information at a later time. This last

point is critical, since if the information is remembered only fleet-
ingly, it is not likely to have any long-lasting impact upon our attitudes or behavior.

Suggestions for Presenting Information Vividly

♦ Research that has investigated public understanding of
resource use demonstrates that the public has a poor understanding of household resource consumption.[5,6]
Householders grossly overestimate the resources used by visible devices such as lighting and greatly underestimate less
visible resource consumption (e.g., water heaters and furnaces). Indeed, in one study homeowners were found to
believe that lighting and hot water heaters consumed an
equivalent amount of energy. This lack of understanding is
reasonable, given the dearth of information that utility bills
provide regarding home resource use. This void of information has been compared to going grocery shopping and dis-
covering that none of the items that you wish to purchase
have price tags.[7] All that you receive when you go through
the checkout is a total for the items purchased. You are left on
your own to estimate the cost of each item. To overcome this
lack of information and the public's bias toward visible
sources of energy use, create a graph that shows the percentage of home energy use by item. Rather than using bars for
the graph, instead replace each bar with a picture of the item
itself (furnace, water heater, major appliances, lighting, etc.). By
presenting information in this vivid format, you enable householders to see clearly where they should be putting most of
their efforts to reduce energy use.

♦ To portray vividly the amount of waste generated by a community, consider using a well-known local landmark. For
example, the amount of waste Toronto generates could be
described relative to the SkyDome.

- Use brightly colored door-hangers rather than flyers or bill inserts. Flyers and bill inserts are frequently ignored. Door hangers that are well designed have a higher likelihood of being noticed.

- To bring attention to the amount of water that is used for lawn watering, prepare a chart like the one described above for energy use that depicts the amount of water consumed for lawn watering, showering, cooking, etc. Lawn watering will dwarf the other items.

- *Life* magazine recently vividly portrayed our consumptive lifestyles by taking all the possessions of an American family and placing them on the front lawn of their house. Next to this picture was a picture of a family from the Third World, once again with all of their possessions placed in front of their home. The contrast in lifestyles and the attendant impacts upon the environment were blatant. In our society, differences in consumption between the wealthy and the poor can be similarly displayed.

Once you have found a way to gain the attention of your intended audience, you next need to consider who your audience is.

Before you craft the content of your message, you need to know the attitudes, beliefs and behaviors of your intended audience.

KNOW YOUR AUDIENCE

Before you craft the content of your message, and decide when and how you will present it, you need to know the attitudes, beliefs and behavior of your intended audience. In reality, rarely do you have just one audience. The messages that you develop will need to be tailored to the different segments of your community that you wish to reach. For example, a program to decrease the purchase of household hazardous waste (HHW) and increase the incidence of household hazardous waste being taken to a depot for disposal might target several different audiences. Preliminary research would need to determine if those who purchase HHW differ based upon the type of product (e.g., household cleaner versus motor oil). Further, you would need to know who would be most likely to collect HHW in the household and who would be most likely to take it to the depot. Clearly, what is seemingly a relatively straightforward program has the potential to have multiple audiences for whom messages will need to be developed. To develop an effective program, therefore, you need to gather as much information as possible about the target audiences to determine how best you can communicate your messages to them. Gathering this type of information is frequently done through the use of surveys and focus groups (see Chapter 2).

A further reason for knowing your audience is provided by the following example. Imagine that you wish to advocate that people adopt simpler, less consumptive lifestyles. You need to know both how receptive people are to such a message and how many people would presently describe themselves as living such a lifestyle. A phone survey can be used to gather this information. Phone surveys and focus groups will also allow you to gauge the level of support for a variety of more and less extreme messages regarding less consumptive lifestyles. In doing this preliminary research, you are trying to find a message that has moderate support. Note that if you have the resources to target your

Know your audience

"Well, I guess I'll have the ham and eggs."

message to different sectors of the community, you will need to determine the level of support within each of these sectors (e.g., the elderly, single parents, etc.). Why concern yourself with finding a message that has general support? Obviously, you don't want a message that is fully supported, or you will simply be communicating what people already believe. However, you do not want to present a message that is too far removed from the beliefs of your audience. If your message is too extreme, your audience will actually become less, rather than more, supportive after hearing your message. In summary, then, you want to tailor your message so that it is slightly more extreme than the beliefs of your audience. Messages that are just slightly more extreme are likely to be embraced. Over time, it is possible to move people's attitudes and beliefs a great deal. However, you will need to have the patience and resources to do this one small step at a time.

USE A CREDIBLE SOURCE

The person who presents your message can have a dramatic impact upon how it is received. In general, the more credible the person or organization delivering the message, the more influence there will be upon the audience.[8] The impact of credibility upon sustainable behavior is demonstrated in a simple, but elegant study. In this study, two groups of homes received an identical pamphlet on energy conservation. In one case, the pamphlet was enclosed in an envelope from the State Regulatory Agency, while in the other the envelope was from the local utility. Prior research had shown that the State Regulatory Agency was viewed as more credible than the local utility, but would simply enclosing the same pamphlet in the two different envelopes have an impact upon home energy use? Yes. Those householders who received the pamphlet from the State Regulatory Agency carried out more of the advocated changes than did the householders who received the identical pamphlet from the local utility.[9]

How do you determine who will be credible for your audience? One method is to use a survey to determine the credibility of several different spokespersons or organizations (see Chapter 2). A simpler method, however, is to search for organizations or individuals who are well known for their expertise in the area and have the public's trust. Perceived credibility appears to be based primarily on these two attributes. You might also consider having your initiative endorsed by a number of credible individuals. Endorsement from several sources is more likely to be effective since some individuals will be more credible to some segments of the public, and other individuals will be more credible to others.

Once you have decided "who" will deliver your message, you next need to concern yourself with "what" will be communicated.

FRAME YOUR MESSAGE

Interestingly, how you present, or "frame," the activity you are trying to promote is very important. Most sustainable activities can be presented positively (You should compost because you'll save in garbage collection user fees), or negatively (If you don't compost you'll lose money by having to pay more to have your garbage collected). Understandably, most organizations gravitate toward presenting positive rather than negative motivations to engage in a new activity. But should they? Apparently, no. Messages which emphasize losses which occur as a result of inaction are consistently more persuasive than messages that emphasize savings as a result of taking action.[10]

CAREFULLY CONSIDER THE USE OF THREATENING MESSAGES

Few public issues lend themselves better to threatening messages than sustainability. Evidence abounds of the predicament we are in. Issues such as species loss, global warming, ozone depletion, and air and water pollution are just a few of the many assaults on the environment and consequently ourselves. However, is it wise to use threatening messages in communicating with the public? There is no simple answer to this question, but here are some of the issues you should consider. First, literature in the field of stress and coping suggests that we need first to appraise an issue as a threat before we are likely to take appropriate action.[11] Rachel Carson's Silent Spring, for example, demonstrates the importance of communicating imminent threats to a wide audience. However,

Threatening or fear arousing messages need to be combined with clear suggestions regarding what people can do to reduce the threat.

to be effective, threatening messages need to communicate more than just the threat we face. In response to a threat, people have what Richard Lazarus refers to as two broad coping strategies. Lazarus' research suggests that individuals respond to threats by using either problem-focused coping or emotion-focused coping. Problem-focused coping, as the name suggests, refers to taking direct action to alleviate the threat. In the case of global warming, problem-focused coping would entail using alternative transportation, increasing the energy efficiency of your home, etc. In contrast, emotion-focused coping might involve ignoring the issue, changing the topic whenever it is raised in conversation, denying that there is anything that can or needs to be done, etc. Whether someone uses problem-focused coping or emotion-focused coping appears to be determined by their perception of how much control they have to right the problem. If we perceive that we have a significant amount of control, we are likely to use problem-focused coping. If we perceive that we have very little, we are likely to use emotion-focused coping. Further, research that I (Doug) have conducted suggests that regarding global issues, our perception of how much control we have is largely determined by our sense of community.[12] If we feel that in concert with others we can have an impact, we are likely to act. If, however, we feel little common purpose, we are likely to perceive that there is little we can do personally.

Messages which emphasize losses that occur as a result of inaction are consistently more persuasive than are messages that emphasize savings as a result of taking action.

Using threatening messages, then, needs to be carefully considered. It is important that your audience understand the gravity of the situation. However, if you are not able at the same time to engender a feeling of common purpose and efficacy in dealing with the threat, your message may cause people to avoid, rather than constructively deal with, the issue.

In summary, threatening messages are a necessary part of directing people's attention to crises. However, they are likely to be counter-productive if they are not coupled with messages that are empowering. Further, repeatedly presenting a threatening message can cause people to become habituated to the message. Once people understand the "crisis," it is wise to move primarily or exclusively on to dealing with the solution.

Decide on a One-Sided versus Two-Sided Message

All issues have more than one side. However, in developing persuasive communication, should you address just one or both sides? The answer, as with most things in life, is "it depends." If you are presenting your communication to an audience that has little comprehension of the issue, you will be most persuasive if you present just one side. However, if you are communicating with an audience that is aware of both sides of the issue, then you need to present both sides to be perceived as credible. As with the content of the message, deciding on a one-sided versus two-sided message once again underscores the importance of knowing your audience.

Presenting two sides of the issue has an additional advantage. By presenting the opposing viewpoint, and providing the counter-arguments to this viewpoint, it is possible to "inoculate" your audience against alternative views.

Finally, where possible, you will want to demonstrate that there is a win-win solution to the problem. Some environmental issues, however, do not lend themselves well to such a solution (e.g., cutting old-growth forest). In these cases, you will likely be best served by presenting both sides of the issue.

MAKE YOUR MESSAGE SPECIFIC

When crafting your message you will want to ensure that the actions that you advocate are clearly articulated. Messages that describe actions to be taken in clear, straightforward steps are more likely to be understood and followed. For example, rather than simply suggesting that households weatherstrip, you need to show clearly each of the steps that are involved in weatherstripping a door or window.

MAKE YOUR MESSAGE EASY TO REMEMBER

All actions that support sustainability require reliance upon memory. Some activities, such as recycling, make substantial demands on memory. In asking someone to recycle, we are requiring them to remember how to recycle (commingled versus separated, whether items have to be washed, etc.), when to recycle, and what to recycle. Research suggests that failing to address the role that memory plays can significantly harm the success of a program.[13] Stuart Oskamp has demonstrated, for example, that recycling programs which make it easy to remember how to recycle, by having the recyclable items commingled rather than separated, have higher participation and substantially higher capture rates (note that this effect might also be due to greater convenience).[14] Further, programs that make it easy to remember when to recycle, by having recycling occur on the same day as garbage collection, also report higher participation rates.[15] Finally, the public can find it quite difficult to remember what to recycle. Many curbside recycling programs have extensive lists of recyclable items. Indeed, when the I (Doug) once asked the project team who had developed the promotional and educational recycling materials for a large municipality to name all of the items that could be recycled, none could. Research suggests that the public knows the main items that can be recycled (glass, cans, newspaper), but has a great deal of difficulty in remembering many other items. In contrast, remembering what to compost is significantly easier. People can create a simple memory device, or heuristic, to guide them in remembering what to compost (if it is food waste or yard waste it is compostable, as long as it is not meat, oil or dairy). In contrast, no simple memory device will work for recycling, since there is no unifying theme that unites all the items.

Unless it is easy for people to remember how, when and what to do, it is unlikely that a program will be successful.

One of the simplest ways to remove the burden that a sustainable activity can place upon memory is through the use of prompts. Remember that to be effective the prompt needs to be presented as close as possible to where the activity is going to occur (see Chapter 4). Affixing a prompt to the side of a blue box meets this criteria of proximity and may be more useful than providing prompts that are affixed to a fridge (it may be advantageous to provide both since some households do not collect recyclables in their blue box). Similarly, attaching a prompt to a kitchen organics catcher can make it easy for people to remember what can be composted, and cut down on contamination rates.

Remember, unless we make it easy for people to remember how, when and what to do, it is unlikely that a program will be very successful.

The major influence on our attitudes and behavior is not the media, but rather our contact with other people.

Provide Personal or Community Goals

Providing targets for a household or a community to reach can be effective in reducing energy and water use and increasing waste reduction. A national survey of the directors of 264 U.S. recycling programs revealed that those cities that had set community recycling goals were more successful than those that had not (clearly, these programs likely differed in other important ways as well).[16]

Emphasize Personal Contact

Research on persuasion demonstrates that the major influence upon our attitudes and behavior is not the media, but rather our contact with other people. That is not to say that the media are without influence. Advertising can be effective in two ways. First, it is effective when the objective is to increase market share by switching the public from one brand of a product to another.[17] Increasing market share is a relatively easy process, given that the consumer is already committed to purchasing a type of product and there are few impediments to altering brand loyalties. Second, the media have an indirect effect by influencing the topics that we discuss. For example, the media may not directly influence you to be more energy efficient. However, if you watch a documentary on global warming, and subsequently discuss it, the conversation you have may convince you to make your home more efficient.

Model Sustainable Behavior

Whether the contact is made personally or through the media, one of the more effective methods for increasing adoption of a sustainable behavior is to model the behavior we wish others to adopt. Modelling involves demonstrating a desired behavior.[18] Modelling can occur in person or through television or videotape. For example, studies have documented significant reductions in energy use in response to either a taped or live broadcast that demonstrated simple conservation methods and mentioned the financial benefits to be gained from carrying them out.[19,20]

Foster Social Diffusion

The adoption of new behaviors, such as recycling and composting, frequently occurs as a result of friends, family members or colleagues introducing us to them. This process is referred to as social diffusion.[21,22,23] Social diffusion has been shown to be a factor in the installation of clock thermostats as well as solar water heaters. While social diffusion appears to be a powerful process, it has been greatly underutilized in attempts to promote sustainable behavior. Two studies discussed earlier demonstrate the potential of social diffusion. Recall that when farmers had received direct assistance with alternative farming practices, they were much more likely to influence others to adopt similar practices than were information-based campaigns. Similarly, homes that made a commitment both to grasscycle and to encourage neighbors to do the same changed not only their own behavior but also the behavior of the neighbors.

In developing a community-based social marketing strategy, look for opportunities to foster social diffusion. One simple method is to advertise the names of people who have made a commitment to carry out a new activity, such as walking to work. By advertising the names not only do you increase the commitment of the individuals whose names are advertised, but you also provide an opportunity for those who recognize someone's name to approach that person and ask about the activity, thereby fostering social diffusion.

Community Block Leaders

Commitment, modelling, norms and social diffusion all have at their core the interaction of individuals in a community. Commitment occurs when one individual pledges to another to carry out some form of activity. Modelling results when we observe the actions of others. Norms develop as people interact and develop guidelines for their behavior, and social diffusion occurs as people pass information to one another regarding their experiences with new activities. Recent research has documented that it is possible to harness these processes in order to have a significant impact upon the adoption of sustainable behaviors. By making use of community volunteers, or block leaders, Shawn Burn has demonstrated the powerful and cost-effective impact that some of these factors can have.[24] Working with city officials in Claremont, California, she arranged to have homes that were not recycling randomly divided into three groups: the first received a persuasive appeal delivered by a block leader, the second received a written persuasive appeal, and the third was a control group. Both the persuasive appeal delivered by the block leader and the written persuasive appeal made use of the same message. The control group homes were not approached and served as a comparison for the other conditions. In the condition in which a persuasive appeal was delivered by a block leader, homeowners were approached by individuals from their community who were already recycling. These "block leaders" delivered a persuasive appeal and left orange recycling bags with the homeowner. In the persuasive message alone condition, homeowners received a written version of the same message and the collection bags. In the 10 weeks that followed the delivery of the messages, the results firmly supported the block leader approach as being most effective. An average of 28% of the homes visited by the block leader recycled weekly, compared with 12% for those who received only the written appeal, and only 3% for the control group. Further, over 58% of those households in the block leader condition recycled at least once in the follow-up, compared with 38% for the written appeal and 19.6% for the control group. The text of the appeal was, as follows:

One of the most effective methods for increasing the adoption of sustainable behavior is to model the behavior we wish others to adopt.

> As a U.S. citizen you probably show your support for our country by voting and paying taxes. Beyond this you may feel that there is nothing more that you can do. However, there are things that you can do. One of these is participation in Claremont's recycling program.
>
> Californians alone produce some 40 million tons of refuse a year — enough to fill a two-lane highway, ten feet deep from Oregon to the Mexican border. Currently, the average person in the U.S. produces about 1,300 lbs. of solid municipal waste a year. Most of this trash goes into landfills, and it is estimated that if present trends continue, nearly all of L.A. County will be without refuse

disposal capacity by 1991. RECYCLING uses wastes instead of filling up landfills. RECYCLING extends resource supplies. RECYCLING IS EASY…SIMPLY PUT NEWSPAPERS, ALUMINUM, AND GLASS INTO SEPARATE BAGS AND PLACE AT THE CURB ON YOUR REGULAR TRASH COLLECTION DAY. Recycling makes a difference and recycling is happening. Over 80% of Claremonters favor the city's recycling program and other cities are calling to ask how Claremont does it. Help us do it, please recycle (Burn, 1991, p. 619-620).

Note how the appeal has made use of several of the principles described above. It has been made vivid (a two-lane highway, ten feet deep from Oregon to the Mexican border), a moderate threat has been used (L.A. County will be without refuse capacity by 1991), the proposed actions are clear and specific (put newspapers, aluminum and glass into separate bags and place at the curb on your regular collection day), the effectiveness of the actions is stressed (recycling makes a difference) and an appeal to norms is made (over 80% of Claremonters favor…). In addition to the content of the message, those that were visited by a block leader would have likely been influenced by several other factors that have been discussed above. For example, the block leader was able to obtain a commitment, served as a model, provided evidence of community norms, and assisted in diffusing the innovation (recycling) throughout the community.

Note that this strategy need not be limited to recycling. It could have similarly been used to promote a variety of activities, such as composting, source reduction, energy conservation or water efficiency.

PROVIDE FEEDBACK

Effective communications involve more than simply presenting information to persuade people to adopt a new activity or making it easy for them to remember what, when and how to do the activity. To be fully effective, information about the impact of newly adopted activities needs to be presented as well. Numerous studies document the impact that providing feedback can have upon the adoption and maintenance of sustainable behavior. Here are several examples:

♦ Posting signs above aluminum can recycling containers that provided feedback about the number of cans that had been recycled during the previous weeks increased capture rates by 65%.[25]

♦ Households were mailed monthly letters that indicated the extent to which they had been able to reduce energy use over the same month during the previous year. In a letter that was sent separately from their bill, they were provided both with the reduction in kWhs and cost. This simple procedure reduced energy use by nearly 5% compared to comparable periods during the previous two years. Further, this study included a control group of households who never received this feedback. During the period of time in which the households who were receiving feedback were reducing energy use, the control households increased energy use.

♦ Households which received daily feedback on the amount of electricity they consumed, lowered energy use by 11% relative to physically identical households who did not receive feedback.[26]

♦ Households which received weekly group feedback on the total pounds of paper they had recycled, increased the amount recycled by 26%.[27] When weekly feedback was combined with public commitments there was a 40% increase.

♦ When residents of the Midland-Odessa (Texas) area were provided with daily evening television feedback and conservation tips, they reduced gasoline usage by 32%.[28] Further, three months after the feedback ended, gasoline usage was 15%

lower than it had been prior to the program.

This chapter has provided a variety of methods by which you can enhance the effectiveness of the communications you produce. In creating future communications, use this checklist as a guide.

A CHECKLIST FOR EFFECTIVE COMMUNICATIONS

♦ Make sure that your message is vivid, personal and concrete.

♦ Using techniques described in Chapter 2, explore the attitudes and behavior of your intended audience prior to developing your message.

♦ Have your message delivered by an individual or organization who is credible with the audience you are trying to reach.

♦ Frame your message to indicate what the individual is losing by not acting, rather than what he/she is saving by acting.

♦ If you use a threatening message, make sure that you couple it with specific suggestions regarding what actions an individual can take.

♦ Use a one-sided or two-sided message depending upon the knowledge of your audience regarding the particular issue.

♦ Make your communication, especially instructions for a desired behavior, clear and specific.

♦ Make it easy for people to remember what to do, and how and when to do it.

♦ Integrate personal or community goals into the delivery of your program.

♦ Model the activities you would like people to engage in.

... more ...

♦ Make sure that your program enhances social diffusion by increasing the likelihood that people will discuss their new activity with others.

♦ Where possible, use personal contact to deliver your message.

♦ Provide feedback at both the individual and community levels about the impact of sustainable behaviors

For examples of *communication* cases and graphics visit www.cbsm.com

Incentives

7

Enhancing Motivation To Act

It is the function of vice to keep virtue
within reasonable bound
— Samuel Butler

When Seattle, Washington, began to charge residents for waste disposal based upon the number of cans of garbage they put at the curbside, the impact was remarkable. Prior to the introduction of user fees in the early 1980's, Seattle residents averaged 3.5 cans of garbage per household each week. By 1992, however, the average number of cans each household put out per week had been reduced to only one.[1] This astonishing decrease was brought about by providing a clear monetary incentive for people to reduce waste and by making it easy for them to divert by recycling.

Incentives, whether financial or otherwise (e.g., social approval), can provide the motivation for individuals to perform more effectively an activity that they already engage in such as recycling, or to begin an activity that they otherwise would not perform, such as composting. This chapter will provide evidence of the impact of incentives in promoting waste reduction, energy efficiency, and alternative transportation. Finally, it will provide some general suggestions on the use of incentives.

INCENTIVES AND WASTE REDUCTION

Incentives have been used primarily to promote waste reduction through two methods: user fees for garbage collection and deposits for beverage containers.

User Fees and Waste Reduction

A growing number of North American cities have implemented user-fee systems for garbage disposal. While significant differences exist in the methods used, reviews of user fee systems clearly indicate that they dramatically reduce the amount of waste going to landfill, and provide additional motivation for households to recycle, compost and, perhaps, source reduce. Here are several examples:

+ When San Jose, California, introduced a user pay program in which residents were charged based upon the size of the container they placed at the curb, the impact was a 46% decrease in waste sent to the landfill, a 158% increase in recyclables captured, and a 38% increase in yard waste collected. There was no charge for curbside recycling and yard waste was collected at the curbside.[2]

+ The Capital Regional District in British Columbia began to charge households for placing more than one bag or container at the curb in January of 1992. Under this program there was a 21% reduction in waste going to the landfill and a 527% increase in recycling capture rates. Curbside recycling was a free service to residents and yard waste had to be taken to a depot.[3]

+ Worchester, Massachusets, introduced a program in which residents purchased bags for their garbage. This program resulted in a 45% reduction in the waste stream, with recycling responsible for 37% of the waste stream diversion. Residents were not charged for recycling nor for dropping off yard waste at a collection center.[4]

+ Sydney Township, Ontario, introduced a user pay system in which residents received 52 free tags to place on garbage bags, with extra tags costing $1.50 Canadian each. Sydney Township carefully monitored the impact that introducing this initiative had upon their waste stream. Relative to the previous year, garbage sent to the landfill was reduced by 46%, weight of blue box recyclables increased by 26%, and the amount of kitchen waste being backyard composted rose by 50%. The introduction of user pay also decreased the amount of HHW placed in garbage by 50%.[5]

Beverage Deposits

Another form of incentive is bottle deposits in which consumers pay an additional charge for purchasing beverages and then receive a portion of the deposit back when they return the container. Several studies indicate that deposits on beverage containers have a substantial impact on littering.

Financial incentives can be powerful tools with which to motivate behavior

♦ The introduction of bottle deposits has been associated with a 68% reduction in litter in Oregon, a 76% reduction in Vermont, and an 82% reduction in Michigan.[6]
♦ When beverage container deposits were introduced in New York State, analysis of a highway exit and a section of a railway track in New York revealed that there was a 74% reduction in litter of stamped 5-cent deposit returnable bottles and cans along the highway exit and 99% reduction along the railway track.[7]

Incentives and Energy Efficiency

Two forms of incentives have been used to promote energy efficiency in residential dwellings; alterations to the price of energy and financial incentives to make a home more energy efficient. Electricity rates in North America have traditionally not favored energy efficiency.[8] Gerald Gardner and Paul Stern note that as home owners and businesses use more energy, the cost they paid decreased, providing little incentive to be efficient (this is referred to as a declining-block rate). Two alternatives to declining-block rates are flat rate systems in which consumers pay the same amount for each kilowatt-hour or "a lifeline rate" in which the cost of electricity increases with greater consumption. A third alternative involves charging higher rates for peak usage times. It costs more to produce electricity at peak usage time due to the need to use additional generating plants, which are often less efficient. Homeowners who have been charged two to eight times as much for peak usage have altered their energy use activities, such as when they run a dishwasher.[9] However, research suggests that peak usage charges need to be carefully explained if they are going to be maximally effective.[10]

Substantial reductions in energy use, from 30 to 50%, are possible if homes are retrofitted to make them more energy efficient. Utilities have offered grants and subsidized loans as incentives to encourage homeowners to invest in energy efficiency retrofits. Qualification for these programs usually requires that a home be subjected to an energy audit. The auditor inspects the home and makes suggestions to the homeowner regarding what improvements should be made to make the home more energy efficient, and provides a grant or loan application and a list of qualified local contractors. Programs such as this have been introduced by a large number of utilities and have produced some consistent findings.[11] In general there is a preference for rebates and grants over loans and, not surprisingly, larger incentives cause larger numbers of households to access a program. Paul Stern and his colleagues have demonstrated that large financial incentives are more likely to result in a retrofit than smaller incentives, but that non-financial factors play an important role in the success of a program. Particularly, it appears that size of the incentive has little impact upon whether a household requests an audit, but has a substantial impact once an audit had been conducted upon whether the homeowners go through with a retrofit. Whether people request audits is influenced primarily by the quality of the communications that are used to advertise the program (see Chapter 6).

INCENTIVES AND TRANSPORTATION

The trends in single-occupant automobile use in North America are distressing. The number of single-occupant cars on the road is increasing and each year those cars are being driven greater distances.[12,13] Automobile use is closely related to pollution in cities as well as to increases in carbon-dioxide (the principal greenhouse gas) in the atmosphere.

To understand the increase in automobile use, it is important to understand the incentives and disincentives that are associated with car travel and its more sustainable alternative, mass transit. Peter Everett and Barry Watson have catalogued the relative incentives and disincentives for these two forms of transportation.[14] Automobile use, they suggest, is associated with shorter travel time, prestige, arrival/departure flexibility, privacy, route selection, cargo capacity, predictability, delayed costs, and enjoyment of driving. Driving a car has a much shorter list of disincentives, including traffic congestion and gas and maintenance costs. In stark contrast, the incentives for mass transit, they suggest, include making friends and having time to read. The disincentives involve exposure to weather, discomfort, noise, dirt, surly personnel, long walks to stops, danger (crime), immediate costs, unpredictability, small cargo capacity, limited route selection, crowds, limited time flexibility, low prestige and long travel time. While Everett and Watson's list is not exhaustive, it nonetheless clearly underscores why so many people elect to drive; compared to the alternatives, the advantages far outweigh the disadvantages.

Companies that match employees based upon the neighborhood they live in can substantially increase car pooling

Steering people away from their reliance upon automobiles depends on altering the balance of incentives and disincentives between driving a car and other more sustainable forms of transportation. A variety of possibilities exist for doing this, many of which have been tried by municipalities in North America and Europe. Numerous communities have introduced laneways that can only be used by multiple-occupant cars or buses. This approach directly targets the convenience of shorter travel times that are associated with single-occupant car use. Similarly, "traffic calming" has been employed in some European cities on residential streets to achieve the same end of increasing the travel time for automobile use. Traffic calming can be accomplished in a variety of ways including converting two-way streets to one-way, reducing the speed limit, or physically altering the design of the street in residential areas to make it more difficult for cars to navigate the street.[15]

In response to the energy crisis in the 1970's, frequent efforts were made by companies to increase car pooling. These efforts often focused on changing the balance of incentives and disincentives for single-occupant car use. In reviewing two of the main strategies in promoting car pooling, Scott Geller and his colleagues found that companies that matched employees with others who lived nearby increased car pooling from 7 to 30%.[16] Providing preferential parking to vehicles that carried multiple passengers was even more effective, increasing ride sharing from 22 to 55%.

Despite these promising results, Gerald Gardner and Paul Stern suggest that there are three incentives that conspire against efforts to promote more sustainable forms of transportation in North America.[17] First, relative to many other countries in the world, the price of gasoline has remained low. Contrary to the trend in Europe of increasing reliance upon mass transit and ever more fuel efficient vehicles, Canada and the United States are moving in the opposite direction. Gardner and Stern report that Europeans pay a minimum of three times as much for gasoline, providing a strong incentive for them to seek alternative forms of transportation, such as railways, which they ride four to eight times as far each year. Second, both the United States and Canada have invested heavily in highway construction that makes it easier for people to live significant distances from where they work. Finally, third, in the United States, but not Canada, interest on mortgages is a tax deduction providing a powerful incentive for people to own single-detached homes in suburbs that are long distances from occupations. These three significant incentives, they suggest, make it difficult to promote alternatives to single occupant car use, and explain why efforts here have focused primarily on making cars more fuel efficient and less polluting rather than on moving people away from their reliance on the automobile.

Creating Effective Incentives

Incentives can be an important component of a community-based social marketing strategy, particularly when motivation to engage in a sustainable behavior is low. Gerald Gardner and Paul Stern have provided guidelines for creating effective incentives (see Gardner and Stern for an in-depth discussion of guidelines for creating effective incentives).[18]

Closely Pair the Incentive and the Behavior

Incentives are usually most effective when they are presented at the time the behavior is to occur. For example, charging for the use of plastic shopping bags at the checkout brings attention to the cost of using disposable bags and increases motivation to bring reusable cotton bags. For example, at the supermarket at which I (Doug) shop, the introduction of a 5 cent charge per plastic bag has resulted in approximately 60% of shoppers using reusable cotton bags or containers for their groceries.

Even small incentives can have dramatic impacts upon behavior

Use Incentives to Reward Positive Behavior

Research in behavior modification underscores the importance of using incentives to reward behavior we would like people to engage in. When sustainable behaviors, such as recycling, are rewarded with lower garbage disposal costs, the likelihood that people will recycle in the future increases. In contrast, disincentives are often less predictable, since the punishment suppresses an unwanted behavior but does not directly encourage a positive alternative. A concrete example of the relative effectiveness of incentives versus disincentives is provided by research in littering which has shown that bottle deposits that reward people for not littering are far more effective than fines that punish people for littering.

Make the Incentive Visible

When implementing an incentive carefully consider how you can draw attention to it. Remember that an incentive will have little or no impact if people are unaware of its existence. For example, the supermarket mentioned above drew attention to the incentive by simply having tellers ask if customers had brought bags from home or if they wished to buy plastic shopping bags. See Chapter 6 on communicating effectively and Chapter 4 on the use of prompts for additional information.

Be Cautious about Removing Incentives

The following story illustrates the importance of keeping incentives in place once they have been introduced:

> A grocer was having difficulty with a group of teenage boys who visited his store each day after school.[19] Shortly after the boys arrived, they would stand outside and verbally abuse the store owner and those who shopped at the store. Indeed, their behavior was so upsetting to some customers that they began to shop elsewhere. Realizing that his business was in jeopardy, the store owner came up with an ingenious plan. The next time the boys arrived, he waited for a few minutes after they began their verbal assault. He then said something that the boys, undoubtedly, thought was remarkable. Rather than criticizing them for their behavior, instead he applauded it. He told the boys that in fact they were so good at yelling obscenities at himself and his customers, he was going to give each of them five dollars. The boys, who likely were beginning to question the sanity of the shop owner, took the money and left shortly thereafter. When they returned the following day, the owner waited once again until

they had hurled insults for a few minutes and then went out and congratulated them on their efforts. He added, however, that the store had not done quite as well as it had yesterday and that all he could afford to give each of them was a dollar. The boys grumbled a little bit, but nonetheless took the money. When they returned the following day, the same events took place, but with the man explaining that he could only afford to give them a quarter each. They grumbled even more, but once again took the money. On the fourth day, he let the boys yell and shout for quite some time before he went out. When he did, he explained that the store had done particularly poorly that day and that he could not afford to pay them anything. Without hesitation the teenagers replied that there was absolutely no way that they were going to yell obscenities each day after school if they were not going to get paid, and left.

This story illustrates the danger of introducing incentives to foster a sustainable behavior and then removing them. Many individuals engage in sustainable activities, such as recycling, because it makes them feel that they are making a positive contribution[18] Similarly, the teenage boys originally showed up at the grocer's store each day after school because they enjoyed being obnoxious. When intrinsic motivations are replaced with incentives, or external motivations, internal motivations can be undermined. Just as the boys intrinsic motivations were jeopardized by the store owner paying them, so can the motivation to recycle be undermined if an incentive is introduced and then removed. In short, think carefully about introducing an incentive, such as user fees, if you believe that the incentive may be removed at some later time.

Prepare for People's Attempts to Avoid the Incentive

Once when driving from Washington to Fredericton, I (Doug) failed to heed the advice of a friend who had told me to give New York City, which falls directly between Washington and Fredericton, a wide berth. As I sat in a line of traffic that barely moved for several hours, I had ample time to observe the car-pool lane in which cars with multiple passengers were speeding by. I noticed that some New Yorkers demonstrated a great deal of ingenuity in avoiding getting stuck in the single-occupant lane, as several cars passed by with well-dressed mannequins riding in the car with them, allowing them to get to their destination quickly, while not having to deal with the inconvenience of carrying passengers with real DNA.

When preparing to use incentives, keep in mind that people can be very creative in avoiding them

When preparing to use incentives keep in mind that people can be very creative in attempting to avoid them. In Victoria, British Columbia, for example, when user fees were introduced for residential garbage collection, some residents would carry their trash downtown and dump it in one of the city street waste baskets. The City of Victoria dealt with this problem by taking out classified ads in the newspaper naming these people and telling them to come down to City Hall to pick up their illegally dumped trash (illegal dumpers frequently left identifying information in their garbage). After running the classified ads for a short time, the practice of "carrying garbage to work" largely stopped[20]

The most effective incentive programs anticipate how people will attempt to avoid engaging in the activity and plan accordingly. For example, bottle deposits demonstrate how an incentive, even when avoided (e.g., someone litters the bottle) can be effective if it motivates someone else to engage in the avoided activity (e.g. to pick up the litter and claim the deposit).

Consider the Size of the Incentive

Incentives need to be large enough to be taken seriously. However, past a certain point diminishing returns occur from increasing the size of the incentive. Study the impact that incentives of different sizes have had in other communities in arriving at the size of incentive for your program.

Consider Non-monetary Forms of Incentives

While financial incentives have received the most attention, other forms of incentives can also be effective. For example, competitions between communities for HHW pick-up days can be used to increase motivation. Similarly, public recognition of individual or organizational actions which foster sustainability can be an important source of motivation.

Examples: Using Incentives to Foster Sustainable Behavior

Waste Reduction

- Place an additional, partially refundable, charge on beverage containers.
- Charge for the use of items such as plastic shopping bags and sytrofoam cups.
- Use user fees to increase motivation to recycle, compost and source reduce.
- Attach a sizable deposit on HHW to provide the motivation necessary for individuals to take leftover products to a depot for proper disposal.

Energy Conservation

- Introduce electricity rates that increase with use.
- Charge variable rates based upon time of use.
- Provide loans, grants or rebates for home energy retrofits.

Water Conservation

- With new meters that can record time of use, charge variable rates based on time of use.
- Provide loans, grants, or rebates to foster the installation of low-flow toilets.

... more ...

TRANSPORTATION

- Decrease the convenience of car travel by reducing speed limits, changing street patterns, and restricting lane use.
- Provide incentives for multiple occupant cars and mass transit by providing exclusive lanes that allow for faster travel times compared to single occupant cars.
- Provide preferential parking for multiple occupant cars.
- Provide matching services that make it easier for people to find other employees with whom they can carpool.

For examples of *incentives* cases and graphics visit www.cbsm.com

Removing
External Barriers

*Everyone confesses in the abstract exertion which brings out all
the powers of body and mind is the best thing for u
all; but practically most people do all they can to get
rid of it, and as a general rule nobody does much
more than circumstances drive them to do.*
— *Harriet Beecher Stowe*

Chapters 3 through 7 identified a variety of tools to overcome an individual's barriers to sustainable behavior. As
powerful as these tools are, they will be ineffective if significant external barriers exist. If the behavior is inconvenient,
unpleasant, costly or time-consuming, for example, no matter how
well you address internal barriers, your community-based social
marketing strategy will be unsuccessful.

The first step to removing external barriers is to identify them.
Using the literature review, focus groups and phone survey techniques outlined in Chapter 2, attempt to isolate what external barriers exist and what can be done to address the barriers you
identify. The City of Boulder, Colorado, for example, identified
twosignificant barriers to mass transit usage: workers' concerns
regarding how they would get home quickly in an emergency
(e.g., a sick child that has to come home from school) and, for
women, safety concerns about taking mass transit late at night.
These two barriers were addressed by providing a free taxi service
in either of these instances.

The role of external barriers is also evident with backyard composting. At present, approximately 30% of homeowners in the
Province of Ontario participate in composting, compared with
over 80% participating in curbside recycling. While many factors

might explain these substantially different participation rates, it is likely that the inconvenience of obtaining a composter, and the perceived inconvenience of composting, are significant barriers. Indeed, in two studies that the first author has conducted in different Canadian cities, inconvenience was on both occasions one of the most significant barriers to composting.[1] Further, in comparing households who compost seasonally with those who compost throughout the year, the only factor which was found to distinguish these two groups was the perceived inconvenience of composting in the winter (remember the anecdote with which I began this book). Communities that provide curbside organic collection effectively eliminate several of the external barriers that exist for backyard composting. First, these communities directly provide households with containers or carts, removing the cost and inconvenience of obtaining a backyard composter from a store. Second, many of these communities provide kitchen organic catchers along with the curbside container, increasing the convenience of collecting organics. Because many of these containers often contain a prompt to identify what can be composted, learning to separate organics is also simplified. Third, unlike backyard composting, the process of curbside organic collection is nearly identical to that used for curbside recycling and garbage disposal (place in a container, take the container to the curb, periodically wash container). The similarity of this new behavior (curbside organic collection) to older, well established behaviors (recycling and garbage collection), simplifies what a household needs to learn in order to participate. The impact of making composting convenient and inexpensive by providing containers and curbside collection can produce dramatic results. In a recent evaluation of a curbside organic pilot, fully 99% of households participated. Indeed, the one household who was not participating, wanted to, but had not received a cart in which to place their organics.

It is important to assess whether it is realistic to overcome the external barriers you identify. To do this, it is useful to explore the success that other programs have had in promoting the same behavior and decide whether you have the resources to mount a similar program. Promoting the use of car pooling, mass transit, bicycling and walking as alternatives to single occupant car usage,

Sustainable activities that are inconvenient usually have low participation rates

as Boulder, Colorado has done, requires significant expenditures. In cases where the financial resources do not exist to make the new behavior more convenient, such as through building bicycle paths, consider instead making the behavior you wish to discourage less convenient and more costly. Multiple possibilities exist for making an activity such as single-occupant driving less convenient and more costly.[2,3] As described in the last chapter, many communities have instituted slower laneways on highways for single-occupant cars or have introduced traffic calming by turning two-way streets into one-way streets. Corporations have discouraged single-occupant car usage by charging more for parking for single-occupant vehicles and making the parking of these cars less convenient (e.g., farther from the building).

Making that activity you wish to discourage less convenient and more expensive can increase motivation for the behavior you wish to encourage. In short, you want to design a program that enhances motivation by making the sustainable behavior more convenient and less costly than the alternative, non-sustainable activity. As demonstrated in the previous chapter, incentives can be effectively used to enhance motivation.

Finally, it is important to note that some external barriers, such as inconvenience, are to some extent a matter of perception. When people have experience with an activity, they often come to see that activity as being more convenient than when they first began. In one study, as individuals gained more experience with recycling bottles they found it more convenient.[4] While strongly "perceived" inconvenience is unlikely to be overcome, tools such as commitment and norms may be used to overcome a more moderate perception of inconvenience.

In summary, because the nature of external barriers can vary dramatically across communities, strategies for removing these barriers will have to be tailored to each situation. Begin by identifying what external barriers exist and then seek information from other communities on how they have dealt with the external barriers you have identified. Next, determine whether you have the resources to implement similar initiatives. If you determine that you do not have the resources, you should seriously reconsider your options. As mentioned above, a community-based social marketing initiative that ignores external barriers is a recipe for failure.

In the box that follows are some external barriers to sustainable behaviors and some possible solutions.

EXAMPLES OF EXTERNAL BARRIERS TO SUSTAINABLE BEHAVIORS

Waste Reduction

♦ It is too inconvenient to obtain a compost unit. Solution: Deliver compost units door-to-door as blue boxes were. When compost units are delivered for free, as they were in a pilot project in the City of Waterloo, Ontario participation

... more ...

rates can rival those for recycling programs.5 In that pilot project, a door hanger was distributed to 300 homes informing residents that they had been selected to receive a free composting unit. Of the 300 homes that were contacted, 253 (or 84%) agreed to accept compost units. In a follow-up survey, 77% of these households were found to be using their compost units.

♦ When inconvenience for office recycling is overcome, the effects can be startling. Providing each office worker with a recycling container for fine paper can increase the amount of fine paper retrieved from a few percent to over 75%.

♦ It is too inconvenient to compost during the winter. Solution: Provide a curbside organic collection during the winter months in which organics are picked up free of charge. Charge during the spring, summer and fall for organic pickup to encourage composting during these months.

♦ It is difficult to identify products that are recyclable or have recycled content. Solution: Provide prompts that make their identification easier (see Chapter 3 on prompts).

♦ The inconvenience of taking household hazardous waste to a depot results in little of this waste being diverted from the landfill. Solution: Provide semi-annual hazardous waste home pick-up dates. Pass a municipal bylaw which mandates that hazardous materials must carry a sticker indicating that the product is a hazardous waste and when the pick-up dates are in that area.

ENERGY CONSERVATION

♦ It is too expensive to upgrade insulation or install energy-efficient windows. Solution: Allow renovations to be paid through savings in energy use. To ensure quality work is

... more ...

done, have contractors provide warranties for energy savings.

♦ Homeowners lack the skills to install energy-efficient devices on their own. Solution: Use home assessments to instruct homeowners on how to install these devices.

WATER CONSERVATION

♦ It is inconvenient to purchase and install toilet dams, faucet aerators and low-flow shower heads. Solution: Have home auditors install these devices during home visits.

♦ For many homes it is too expensive to install a low-flow toilet. Solution: Allow the cost of the toilet and installation to be paid for from savings in the water bill.

TRANSPORTATION

♦ It is inconvenient to use mass transit compared to driving a car. Solution: Alter the relative convenience by making driving less convenient (e.g., slower laneways for single-occupant cars, introduce traffic calming and one-way streets).

For examples of *external barriers* cases and graphics visit www.cbsm.com

Design & Evaluation
Building Effective Programs

9

The great tragedy of Science - the slaying of a beautiful
hypothesis with an ugly fact.
— *T.H. Huxley*

If a program is to be effective, careful consideration needs to be given to strategy development. This chapter will clarify how to design, pilot, implement and evaluate a community-based social marketing strategy.

The development of a strategy begins with identifying barriers and benefits to the desired activity, using the tools described in Chapter 2. This identification is followed by strategy development. Once the strategy is complete, the next step is to conduct focus groups to obtain reactions to the proposed strategy. If the strategy receives positive reviews, you are ready to pilot. If not, you will want to make further refinements. In the pilot, you test the effectiveness of the strategy with a limited number of people. Essentially, you want to know, before you commit to using the strategy throughout a community, that it will work effectively. If the pilot is successful, you can be much more confident of success when you broadly implement the strategy. If the pilot is unsuccessful, then you need to make further revisions, and pilot again before broad-scale implementation and evaluation.

As can be seen above, the design of a community-based social marketing strategy is pragmatic; each step builds on those that precede it. Effective design will not only help ensure the success of a program, but can also serve one other important purpose; cementing funding support. Increasingly, funders are demanding that projects have a solid research foundation and be piloted before being implemented. The tools introduced in this chapter can help you to persuade your funders that your initiative is worth supporting.

DESIGN AND EVALUATION: AN EXAMPLE

To introduce the design and evaluation of a community-based social marketing strategy, a hypothetical program to foster the purchase of products with recycled-content will be used. Following this example, critical elements of design and evaluation will be outlined..

Imagine that preliminary research (see Chapter 2) has identified the following barriers to consumers purchasing products that have recycled-content:

♦ products are viewed as difficult to identify;
♦ shoppers forget to consider whether a product has recycled-content; and
♦ buying recycled-content products is not seen as the "right thing to do."

Knowing that recycled-content products are difficult to identify suggests that prompts should be effective in promoting these purchases (see Chapter 4). That consumers forget to consider these properties when making a purchase also suggests that prompts may be an effective tool in promoting the purchase of products with recycled-content. Finally, that buying these products is not seen as the "right thing to do" clarifies that an effective strategy will need to foster supportive norms (see Chapter 5).

What might a community-based social marketing strategy look like which incorporates these behavior change tools? As mentioned in Chapter 4, prompts are most effective when presented at the time the activity is to occur. To encourage the purchase of recycled-content products, prompts would be placed on the store shelves directly below these items. To assist shoppers in easily identifying these products, a graphic design that visually suggests the importance of purchasing products with recycled-content would be used (see Chapter 4 for an example of such a prompt). The prompt would also contain a brief explanation of why buying products with recycled-content is important (remember that for a prompt to be effective, it needs to contain all of the information that is necessary for someone to act appropriately).

Occasionally it is possible to overcome two barriers to a sustainable behavior with one tool. In encouraging shoppers to select products that have recycled-content, the use of prompts makes it significantly easier to identify these products (the first barrier) and increases the likelihood that shoppers will remember to consider these characteristics (the second barrier).

How might community norms be established that foster purchasing recycled-content products? At the beginning of the promotion, asking shoppers to wear a sticker or button that said "I buy recycled" would likely help to establish the community norms discussed in Chapter 5.† Asking shoppers to wear a sticker or button not only assists in establishing these norms, but also bolsters commitment (see Chapter 3). Since people wish to behave consistently, agreeing to wear a button or sticker increases the likelihood that they will purchase recycled-content products.

Posters clarifying the meaning of these prompts, or "shelf talkers," would be placed prominently throughout the store (particularly near entrances) In addition, pamphlets at checkouts and potentially a mobile video kiosk would be used to educate shop-

---

† Asking shoppers to wear a sticker or a button as they enter the store will not only help to establish a norm favouring the purchase of these products and build commitment, but will also serve to highlight the campaign for these shoppers. Nonetheless, the sticker and button will only be worn for a short time before it will be removed. A more permanent way to establish community norms that support the purchase of these products is to ask householders to place a sticker on the side of their blue box that indicates that the household shops for recycled or recyclable products. The development of community norms can also be facilitated through the use of block leaders (see Chapter 6: Communication) who seek commitments from householders to purchase products that favour the environment and indicate how to go about doing so.

pers about the importance of selecting products with these characteristics.

The proposed social marketing strategy deals with each of the identified barriers to purchases of products with these characteristics. However, simply selecting and incorporating the tools discussed in this book into a community-based social marketing strategy will not ensure its success. Prior to implementing a strategy throughout a community, it should be tested through focus groups and a pilot.

Focus Groups

While focus groups, as explained in Chapter 2, can be used to explore barriers to a behavior, focus groups can also provide useful information on the appeal and acceptance of a proposed strategy. To obtain feedback on the above strategy, several focus groups of five to six individuals would be conducted. For each focus group, the purpose of the campaign would be explained and participants would be introduced to drafts of the proposed prompts, stickers (buttons), brochures, posters and video.† Focus group participants would be asked whether these materials would capture their attention and if they are clear and easy to understand (see Chapter 6). Once feedback has been received on these characteristics of the materials, participants would be asked if they perceived any difficulties with the proposed strategy and if they had any suggestions for how it could be strengthened.

Following completion of the focus groups, responses to the proposed strategies would be tabulated to uncover any potential themes in participants' responses Where warranted, the strategy would be refined based on the feedback received. After the strategy has been refined, the pilot is conducted.

---

† Given the cost and time involved in producing a video, focus groups can be asked to review the story-boards that precede the development of the video rather than the video itself.

Pilot

Think of the pilot as a "test run," an opportunity to work out the "bugs" before committing to carrying out a strategy across a community. To pilot the above strategy, the store managers of two supermarkets would be approached and asked if they would be willing to participate. The two stores would need to be similar both in the demographics of their shoppers as well as in the products available (two stores of the same chain would be good candidates). By the flip of a coin, one of the stores would be randomly assigned to receive the community-based social marketing strategy, while the other would serve as a comparison (what is referred to as a control).

Prior to piloting the strategy, the rate of purchase for recycled-content products would be determined by examining the computerized inventory records for these items. Note that it is important to collect this data for both stores, since they may differ initially from one another. Also it is important to obtain this baseline data for a sufficient period of time (usually a month or more). Following the baseline period, the prompts, posters, buttons (stickers), pamphlets and video kiosk would be introduced in the intervention store. After introducing the strategy, the rate of purchase of targeted items would be monitored for several months to ascertain if the strategy produces a sustained impact upon the purchase of these products.

To determine whether the strategy alters consumer purchases, the purchase of the targeted items during the baseline period is compared to purchases during the intervention (seasonal adjustments may need to be made to these numbers to control for increased purchases around events such as Christmas). The success of the strategy cannot simply be determined by comparing the purchases of the targeted items for the two stores. The following example clarifies how to determine correctly the impact of the strategy. Imagine that after implementing the above strategy, the "intervention" store had sold 5000 units of recycled-content toilet paper, while the control store had sold only 3000. On first glance it appears that the community-based social marketing strategy has brought about a 67% increase in sales for this one item. However, such a conclusion assumes that the stores initially sold an equal amount of recycled-content toilet paper, which is very unlikely. To determine the "real" impact of the intervention, the sales of toilet paper during the baseline period for both stores needs to be considered. Imagine that baseline data revealed that the intervention store had sold in the month prior to the intervention 2500 units of toilet paper and the control store had sold 2000. The real increase in sales that can be attributed to the intervention, 50%, would be determined as follows:

Intervention : 5000 (intervention period) - 2500 (baseline
                period) = 2500
Control :   3000 (intervention period) - 2000 (baseline
                period) = 1000
Real Impact: 2500 - 1000 = 1500

If, when comparing inventory records prior to and following the implementation of the intervention, little or no change in consumer purchases is observed, then the pilot would need to be revised until significant changes in behavior were observed. Since in this proposed initiative the prompts are a central aspect of the campaign, it is natural to start by investigating them. By conducting in-store surveys with a random selection of shoppers, awareness and understanding of the prompts could be probed. If low recognition and understanding of the prompts was observed, then the prompts would need to be redesigned to be more prominent and clear. Further, the placement of the posters which explain the purpose of the shelf talkers should be examined. Did shoppers recall seeing the poster? Did they know what the posters said? If the answer to either of these questions is no, it is possible that simply changing the location and/or number of posters might address this problem. The point of the pilot is to identify and address these problems before launching the campaign throughout the community. You should plan on there being problems and build into your plans the opportunity to refine your strategy until it works well. On one project, I (Doug) revised a pilot six times before I was able to produce the desired changes in behavior While it was frustrating to have to make this many revisions, I was thankful that I was making the revisions to a pilot rather than to a larger project, for which the problems would have been much more difficult and expensive to rectify. Expect problems, plan for them; in the end, when you implement community-wide you will be rewarded for the time that you took to trouble-shoot.

Community Implementation and Evaluation

When the pilot has successfully demonstrated that the purchase of these products can be substantially increased by the community-based social marketing strategy, it is ready to be implemented across the community. In implementing the initiative, advertising and local media can be used to create additional awareness that would have been undesirable during the pilot In implementing this initiative throughout the community, limited advertising resources could be leveraged by creating public awareness through hosting media events both to launch the campaign and to provide feedback on its success. Further, participating retailers could be encouraged to advertise the campaign in their own advertising, greatly increasing exposure (this is a requisite for some levels of involvement in the "Buy Recycled" campaign discussed in Chapter 4).

When implementing throughout the community, it is also

important to build in a method to evaluate the impact of the initiative. In the hypothetical project described here, a random selection of retailers would be selected to participate in the evaluation. Baseline data from the electronic inventories of these stores would be obtained and then compared to changes that occurred in the purchase of the targeted products following the launch of the campaign. To provide a stable picture of the impact that this campaign had upon the purchase of these products, the average increase in the purchase of these products across the evaluated stores would be determined. This information not only serves as a critical test of the success of the initiative, but serves two other important functions. First, it is important to provide the community with feedback (see Chapter 6) regarding the impact that their changes in behavior has upon the environment. In other words, an element of a successful community-based social marketing strategy is providing feedback that reinforces the changes that people have made. The media will often provide you with a cost-effective way of getting this information back to consumers, though other possibilities exist. One vivid and ongoing form of feedback is to provide shoppers in each retail store with a yardstick of their efforts. By setting up a display in which the percentage increase in the purchase of these products is updated on a regular basis, shoppers can be provided with an ongoing source of feedback and encouragement (the use of feedback can also help to establish a norm that favors this form of shopping). Second, as mentioned at the beginning of this chapter, program evaluation provides evidence of concrete results, which is most convincing to funders that a campaign is worth continued support.

DESIGN AND EVALUATION PRINCIPLES

The preceding example demonstrated many of the critical aspects of designing and evaluating a community-based social marketing strategy. This section provides an overview of design and evaluation principles.

Begin with Barriers: The development of any community-based social marketing strategy begins with the identification of barriers. Using the methods outlined in Chapter 2, identify barriers to the activity you wish to promote prior to giving further consideration to designing a strategy. As you identify barriers, keep in mind that most activities consist of a variety of component behaviors. You need to know the barriers for each of these component behaviors if your strategy is to be effective.

Prioritize the Barriers: In identifying the barriers, use statistical analysis (multivariate approaches) to help you clarify which barriers are the most significant. It is likely that your research will identify a number of barriers and you will want to ensure that your limited resources are spent on overcoming the most important barriers.

Select Tools that Match Identified Barriers: To design an effective strategy, it is essential that the tools you select are tailored to the barriers you encounter. For example, if motivation appears to be a problem, consider the use of commitment (Chapter 3) or incentives (Chapter 7). If few people perceive the activity as the "right thing to do," you will likely want to develop community norms using some of the strategies that are discussed in Chapter 5. If there is a lack of awareness or knowledge regarding the activity, you will want to incorporate many of the tools of effective communication that are discussed in Chapter 6.

> *Closely match the tools you use to the barriers you identify*

Scrutinize your Design with Focus Groups: Prior to piloting your strategy, conduct focus groups to receive feedback on your proposed strategy. The information you obtain from these focus groups will often assist you in designing a more effective strategy.

Use a Minimum of Two Groups to Conduct your Pilot: When you conduct your pilot, you want to make sure that any changes you observe are the result of your intervention and not other events that are occurring in the community. To be certain that it is your intervention that is bringing about the changes you observe, always include a control group to which nothing is done. By comparing your intervention and control groups, you can be much more confident that your intervention was responsible for any changes you observe.

GUIDELINES FOR SELECTING CONSULTANTS

You may wish to contract out the design, implementation and evaluation of your program. Here are some suggestions to increase the likelihood that you end up with a consultant who has the necessary skills to use community-based social marketing. In the request for proposals ask that proposals:

- ♦ **be based upon community-based social marketing methods;**
- ♦ **specify how barriers to the activity will be identified;**
- ♦ **clarify what behavior change tools might be used (e.g., commitment, prompts, norms, social diffusion, etc.);**
- ♦ **indicate how the strategy will be piloted;**
- ♦ **specify how the program will be evaluated once implemented throughout the community ;**
- ♦ **provide evidence of competence in survey design, research design and data analysis (at least one member of the research team should have graduate level training in research methods and statistics); and**
- ♦ **provide evidence of familiarity with designing and implementing community-based social marketing strategies.**

You may wish to have more than two groups. For example, as in many of the studies described in this book, you may wish to have one group receive a commitment strategy, a second receive feedback, a third receive a combination of the two, and a fourth act as a control. Keep in mind that pilots can often be quite inexpensive to conduct since the size of groups can be kept small (30 to 40 residences each). Including multiple groups in your pilot can help you determine the form that your strategy will take when you implement it across your community. For example, as a result of conducting a pilot on fostering car pooling, you may learn that obtaining commitments provides no additional benefit over assisting employees in identifying others who live in their neighborhood with whom they might drive to work. As a result, your subsequent program would drop commitment as part of the strategy.

Use Random Assignment: When you conduct a pilot, you want to know that the group that receives your intervention is as nearly identical as possible to the group that serves as the control. The only way that you can assume this is if the people are randomly assigned to one group or another. To randomly assign individuals or households to the groups you plan to use, simply place the names or addresses of all individuals in a hat and then pull them out assigning, the first person or address to the first group, the second to the second group, etc.

Make Measurements of Behavior Change a Priority: In evaluating the effectiveness of a pilot, your primary concern should always be whether you were able to change the behavior that you set out to change. Where possible, don't rely upon people's self reports of their behavior; they can be unreliable. Obtain water records, ask to look in composters, examine weather-stripping, etc. You will also want to examine people's perceptions and attitudes, but don't see these as substitutes for examining actual changes in behavior.

Revise your Pilot Until it is Effective: It is tempting when a pilot is ineffective to assume that you know what went wrong and move directly to community-wide implementation. Keep in mind that pilots can often be conducted very quickly. Take the time to run another pilot to confirm that you are actually able to change behavior before you implement across a community. The extra time that you take to run the pilot may save you hundreds of thousands of dollars if your intuition has betrayed you.

Evaluate the Community Implementation: Prior to conducting your community-wide implementation, collect baseline information about the rate at which people are presently engaging in the activity you wish to promote. Where possible, use actual observations of behavior or reliable records (e.g., water meter readings) rather than self-reports to establish this baseline. Once you have implemented your program, begin to collect data to ascertain its impact. Keep in mind that you will want to conduct these evaluations at different time intervals.

PUBLIC CONSULTATION

Community-based social marketing is based heavily upon public consultation. As explained previously, the process of designing a strategy involves obtaining information from the community at three separate times. First, just after conducting the literature review, focus groups are conducted to obtain in-depth information on perceived barriers to the behavior you wish to promote. Second, this information is supplemented by the phone survey, which provides more information about perceived barriers, attitudes and present levels of involvement in the activity. Third, the social marketing strategy is reviewed by another series of focus groups who provide feedback on the planned strategy. These three steps help ensure that the strategy you devise will be well tailored to your community.

This consultation should be part of the development of any community-based social marketing strategy. However, you may wish to add another opportunity for public involvement - active participation in determining the initial marketing strategy. Some organizations create a stakeholder consultation committee for this purpose. Whether you elect to create a stakeholder consultation committee, and if you do, when they become involved in the process is a matter of personal preference. My own preference (Doug) is to create a stakeholder committee whenever the planned program is likely to be of special interest or concern (e.g., implementing user fees for garbage disposal), or when the activity you are attempting to promote is not well understood and hence you need input from as many sources as possible. It is often not necessary to create a stakeholder committee when neither of these two criteria are met.

If you decide to form a stakeholder committee, it can be formed at the outset (e.g., prior to the literature review) or after information from the literature review, focus groups and phone survey have been conducted. Once again, when you decide to form the committee is a matter of personal preference. I prefer to create the committee at the outset if the program has any potential to be controversial, in order to circumvent concerns about decisions being made without public input. On the other hand, early creation of the committee can make some initial parts of collecting information on barriers, such as the survey, torturous if not well managed. Don't place yourself in the position of writing a phone survey by committee. Do seek suggestions about potential topics that should be addressed in the survey, but avoid having the survey reviewed by the stakeholder committee.

No matter when you involve a stakeholder committee, you will need to decide beforehand what constraints will be placed upon the committee. For example, if council has made it clear that no subsidies will be provided for the installation of low-flow toilets, your committee needs to know at the outset what limitations have been placed upon the strategies that can be considered. If you are going to be acting as a facilitator for stakeholder meetings, remain impartial when receiving feedback from participants. Your role is to encourage constructive input on the design of a strategy. Remaining impartial will facilitate receiving the broadest feedback.

THE FINAL REPORT: GETTING THE WORD OUT

After conducting a literature review, running focus groups, writing, conducting and analyzing a phone survey, devising a strategy, scrutinizing it with focus groups and a stakeholder committee, piloting the strategy, revising the strategy, implementing it throughout the community and evaluating it, you should be finished, right? Wrong. Community-based social marketing is an emerging field that holds great promise for moving us toward a sustainable future. Take the time to write up a final report and make sure that people know about it. Whether your community-based social marketing strategy was successful or not, others need to learn from your efforts. Please consider adding a description of your project to the case studies database that can be found at www.cbsm.com. To do this, simply go to the case studies section of the site and use the online form to enter a description of your project. Once entered, your description is available for review by anyone who designs environmental programs and has access to the internet.

Concluding Thoughts

10

By persuading others, we convince ourselves.
— *Junius (18th century)*

A friend who designs ICI waste reduction strategies for a regional municipality told me that while he was reading a draft of this book he grew increasingly uncomfortable. His discomfort, he explained, came from realizing that the tools and strategies set out here are more effective than the ones he was presently using and that he would have to change how he designed and delivered programs. He went on to explain that using community-based social marketing would involve relearning important aspects of his job and that he had grown comfortable with the tools that he has used for some time. Resistance to using community-based social marketing, he correctly pointed out, has to be overcome even by those who believe in its utility.

OVERCOMING RESISTANCE IN YOURSELF

Clearly, the tools and strategies detailed in this book will initially require more work. Implementing a community-based social marketing strategy requires careful preliminary research, strategy development, piloting, implementation and evaluation. However, this attention to detail is in large part why community-based social marketing is often so successful. Following the steps described here can greatly increase the likelihood of your program being successful. For example:

- the literature review allows your program to build on the work of others;
- the focus groups and phone survey allow you to determine

what barriers will need to be overcome in order to design an effective community-based social marketing strategy;

◆ piloting the strategy will allow you to test its impact and further refine the strategy to increase its effectiveness; and

◆ evaluating the program once it has been implemented across the community will allow you to speak with confidence regarding its impact and provide you with the data you need to ensure continued funding.

Program design and evaluation are critical components of community-based social marketing, but they are not unique to it. Increasingly, program design and evaluation are being mandated for a wide range of social programs. As governments are increasingly held accountable for the wise use of tax dollars, program design and evaluation will become the norm rather than the exception. Further, over time program design and evaluation reduce the cost and effort that has to be expended to foster sustainable behavior. Programs that are not properly designed and evaluated are frequently less effective. As a consequence, several programs often have to be developed and delivered to bring about the same change in behavior as one well designed program. In short, properly designing and evaluating a community-based social marketing strategy will initially entail more work on your part, but this effort will be rewarded both through greater impact and lower long-term costs.

Overcoming Resistance Among Colleagues

The approaches detailed in this book are new and may be seen as unproven by your colleagues. How can you overcome their resistance? It will help if you prepare for some of the problems that you might encounter.

You will need to be prepared to deal with concerns your colleagues will have over the length of time that it will take to design and implement a community-based social marketing strategy. You will need to reassure them that the approaches outlined here are more likely to succeed, and as a result, resources and staff will be used more responsibly and effectively. Additionally, be prepared that some of your colleagues may not want to evaluate programs for fear that evaluation might produce negative results. You may also encounter resistance to community-based social marketing since using these approaches may be seen by some colleagues as an implicit admission that past initiatives were not designed as effectively as they might have been.

Here are some suggestions for increasing support for community-based social marketing in your organization:

♦ Ask colleagues to read this book;
♦ Bring in a speaker to introduce community-based social marketing to your organization;
♦ Distribute articles that demonstrate the effectiveness of community-based social marketing strategies (references for all of the studies described here follow this chapter, an even more comprehensive and up-to-date listing can be found at www.sustainable.stthomasu.ca);
♦ Ask someone who has successfully implemented a community-based social marketing strategy to come and speak to your organization about it;
♦ Ask that current programs be rigorously evaluated and that the evaluation focus on behavior change rather than awareness of marketing messages. It is easy to believe that a program is working if little or no concrete data exists to measure its success.

Be prepared that it may take a considerable length of time to overcome resistance from your colleagues. Indeed, you may put forward several community-based social marketing proposals only to find each of them rejected. Remember, as you advocate with resistant colleagues, you are slowly creating new norms regarding how programs should be carried out. You can be confident that eventually community-based social marketing strategies will replace the more traditional approaches discussed in Chapter 1 for one simple reason: they are more effective.

GOING FORWARD

As we move rapidly toward a world with twice today's inhabitants, and ever dwindling renewable resources, the tools and methods described here will become increasingly important. Community-based social marketing holds great promise in promoting sustainable behavior. The speed with which community-based social marketing supplants less effective traditional approaches will depend, however, upon the quick dissemination of successes and failures in using this new approach. As discussed in the chapter on effective communication, the adoption of new lifestyles is often the result of social diffusion. Similarly, the adoption of new techniques, such as community-based social marketing, occurs primarily through the informal sharing of information. I (Doug) encourage you to discuss your efforts in using these new techniques with others, and to make use of the on-line discussion forum that can be found at www.cbsm.com. Through this forum, you have the opportunity to share your successes and failures in the use of community-based social marketing, and to learn from the experiences of others who are tackling similar problems. Each time we share information and refine our techniques, we collectively become a little wiser and move a small step closer to the sustainable future our children deserve.

Using these approaches may be seen by some colleagues as an implicit admission that past initiatives were not as well designed as they might have been

References

Preface

[1] United Nations Population Fund. (1991). *Population, resources and the environment: The critical challenges.* New York: Author.

[2] Olson, R. (1995). Sustainability as a social vision. *Journal of Social Issues, 51,* 15-36.

[3] Aronson, E., & Gonzales, M.H. (1990). Alternative social influence processes applied to energy conservation. In J. Edwards, R. S. Tindale, L. Heath, & E. J. Posaval (Eds.), *Social Influences, Processes and Prevention* (pp. 301-325). New York: Plenum.

[4] Costanzo, M., Archer, D., Aronson, E., & Pettigrew, T. (1986). Energy conservation behavior: The difficult path from information to action. *American Psychologist, 41,* 521-528.

[5] Yates, S.M., & Aronson, E. (1983). A social psychological perspective on energy conservation in residential buildings. American Psychologist, 38, 435-444.

[6] Andreasen, A. R. (1995). *Marketing social change: Changing behavior to promote health, social development, and the environment.* San Francisco: Jossey Bass.

[7] Gonzales, M. H., Aronson, E., & Costanzo, M. A. (1988). Using social cognition and persuasion to promote energy conservation: A quasi-experiment. *Journal of Applied Social Psychology, 18,* 1049-1066.

[8] Burn, S. M. (1991). Social psychology and the stimulation of recycling behaviors: The block leader approach. *Journal of Applied Social Psychology, 21,* 611-629.

Chapter 1: Fostering Sustainable Behavior

[1] Kasturi Rangan, V., Karim, S. & Sandberg, S. K. (1996). Doing better at doing good. *Harvard Business Review, May-June,* 42-54.

[2] For a healthy nation: *Returns on investments in public health.* U.S. Department of Health and Human Services.

[3] For a healthy nation: *Returns on investments in public health.* U.S. Department of Health and Human Services

[4] Geller, E.S. (1981). Evaluating energy conservation programs: Is verbal report enough? *Journal of Consumer Research, 8,* 331-335.

[5] Midden, C. J., Meter, J. E., Weenig, M. H., & Zieverink, H. J. (1983). Using feedback, reinforcement and information to reduce energy consump-

tion in households: A field-experiment. Journal of Economic Psychology, 3, 65-86.

6 Jordan, J. R., Hungerford, H. R., & Tomera, A. N. (1986). Effects of two residential environmental workshops on high school students. *Journal of Environmental Education, 18,* 15-22.

7 Geller, E. S., Erickson, J. B., & Buttram, B. A. (1983). Attempts to promote residential water conservation with educational, behavioral, and engineering strategies. *Population and Environment, 6,* 96-112.

8 Tedeschi, R. G., Cann, A., & Siegfried, W. D. (1982). Participation in voluntary auto emissions inspection. *Journal of Social Psychology, 117,* 309-310.

9 Bickman, L. (1972). Environmental attitudes and actions. *Journal of Social Psychology, 87,* 323-324.

10 Finger, M. (1994). From knowledge to action? Exploring the relationships between environmental experiences, learning, and behavior. *Journal of Social Issues, 50,* 141-160.

11 Archer, D., Pettigrew, T., Costanzo, M., Iritani, B., Walker, I. & White, L. (1987). Energy conservation and public policy: The mediation of individual behavior. *Energy Efficiency: Perspectives on Individual Behavior,* 69-92.

12 De Young, R. (1989). Exploring the difference between recyclers and non-recyclers: The role of information. *Journal of Environmental Systems, 18,* 341-351.

13 Costanzo, M., Archer, D., Aronson, E., & Pettigrew, T. (1986). Energy conservation behavior: The difficult path from information to action. *American Psychologist, 41,* 521-528.

14 Hirst, E. (1984). Household energy conservation: A review of the federal residential conservation service. *Public Administration Review, 44,* 421-430.

15 Hirst, E., Berry, L., & Soderstrom, J. (1981). Review of utility home energy audit programs. *Energy, 6,* 621-630.

16 Hirst, E. (1984). Household energy conservation: A review of the federal residential conservation service. *Public Administration Review, 44,* 421-430.

17 U.S. Department of Energy (1984). *Residential conservation service evaluation report: Hearings before the Committee on Energy and Natural Resources of the United States Senate, Ninety-Eighth Congress).* Washington, D.C.: U.S. Government Printing Office; Hirst, E. (1984).

Household energy conservation: A review of the federal residential conservation service. *Public Administration Review, 44,* 421-430; Hirst, E., Berry, L., & Soderstrom, J. (1981). Review of utility home energy audit programs. *Energy, 6,* 621-630.

[18] Stern, P.C., & Aronson, E. (Eds.). (1984). Energy use: *The human dimension.* New York: Freeman.

[19] Larson, M. A. & Massetti-Miller, K. L. (1984). Measuring change after a public education campaign. *Public Relations Review, 10,* 23-32.

[20] Pope, E. (1982, December 10). PG&E's loans aimed at poor miss the mark. *San Jose Mercury,* p. 6B.

[21] Costanzo, M., Archer, D., Aronson, E., & Pettigrew, T. (1986). Energy conservation behavior: The difficult path from information to action. American Psychologist, 41, 521-528.

[22] Costanzo, M., Archer, D., Aronson, E., & Pettigrew, T. (1986). Energy conservation behavior: The difficult path from information to action. *American Psychologist, 41,* 521-528.

[23] Stern, P.C., & Oskamp, S. (1987). Managing scarce environmental resources. In D. Stokols, & I. Altman (Eds.), *Handbook of environmental psychology* (pp. 1043-1088). New York: Wiley.

[24] McKenzie-Mohr, D., Nemiroff, L. S., Beers, L., & Desmarais, S. (1995). Determinants of responsible environmental behavior. *Journal of Social Issues, 51,* 139-156.

[25] Oskamp, S., Harrington, M.J., Edwards, T.C., Sherwood, D.L., Okuda, S.M., & Swanson, D.C. (1991). Factors influencing household recycling behavior. *Environment and Behavior, 23,* 494-519; and Tracy, A.P., & Oskamp, S. (1983-84). Relationships among ecologically responsible behaviors. *Journal of Environmental Systems, 13,* 115-126.

Chapter 2: Uncovering Barriers to Behavior

[1] Sudman, S. & Bradburn, N.M. (1982). Asking questions: A practical guide to questionnaire design. San Francisco: Jossey-Bass.

[2] National Recycling Coalition, 1727 King St., Alexandria, Virginia, 22314, (703) 683 9025, (703) 683 9026 fax; Recycling Council of Ontario, 489 College St., Suite 504, Toronto, Ontario, M6G 1A5, (416) 960 1025, (416) 960 8053 fax; The Waste Watch Centre, 16 Haverill St., Andover, Mass., U.S. 01810, (508) 470 3044.

[3] Archie, M., Mann, L. & Smith, W. A. (1993). *Partners in action: Environmental social marketing and environmental education,* Washington, D.C.: Academy for Educational Development.

[4] Fishbein, M. & Middlestadt, S.E. (1989) Using the theory of reasoned action as a framework for understanding and changing AIDS-related behaviors. In V.M. Mays, G.W. Albee, S.F. Schneider (Eds.), *Primary Prevention of Aids* (pp. 93-110), London: Sage.

[5] McKenzie-Mohr, D., Nemiroff, L.S., Beers, L. & Desmarais, S. (1995). Determinants of responsible environmental behavior, *Journal of Social Issues, 51*, 139-156.

Chapter 3: Commitment

[1] Freedman, J.L., & Fraser, S. C. (1966). Compliance without pressure: The foot-in-the-door technique. *Journal of Personality and Social Psychology, 4,* 195-202.

[2] Freedman, J.L., & Fraser, S. C. (1966). Compliance without pressure: The foot-in-the-door technique. *Journal of Personality and Social Psychology, 4,* 195-202.

[3] Schwarzwald, J., Raz, M., & Zvibel, M. (1979). The efficacy of the door-in-the-face technique when established behavioral customs exist. *Journal of Applied Social Psychology, 9,* 576-586.

[4] Sherman, S. J. (1980). On the self-erasing nature of errors of prediction. *Journal of Personality and Social Psychology, 39,* 211-221.

[5] Greenwald, A.G., Carnot, C.G., Beach, R., & Young, B. (1987). Increasing voting behavior by asking people if they expect to vote. *Journal of Applied Psychology, 72,* 315-318.

[6] Lipsitz, A., Kallmeyer, K., Ferguson, M., & Abas, A. (1989). Counting on blood donors: Increasing the impact of reminder calls. *Journal of Applied Social Psychology, 19,* 1057-1067.

[7] Pliner, P., Hart, H., Kohl, J., & Saari, D. (1974). Compliance without pressure: Some further data on the foot-in-the-door technique. *Journal of Experimental Social Psychology, 10,* 17-22.

[8] Cialdini, R. B. (1993). *Influence: Science and practice.* New York, NY: HarperCollins College Publishers.

[9] Moriarty, T. (1975). Crime, commitment, and the responsive bystander. *Journal of Personality and Social Psychology, 31,* 370-376.

[10] Gonzales, M.H., Aronson, E., & Costanzo, M.A. (1988). Using social cognition and persuasion to promote energy conservation: A quasi-experiment. *Journal of Applied Social Psychology, 18,* 1049-1066.

[11] Shippee, G. E., & Gregory, W. L. (1982). Public commitment and energy conservation. American *Journal of Community Psychology, 10,* 81-93.

[12] Hutton, R.R. (1982). Advertising and the Department of Energy's cam-

paign for energy conservation. *Journal of Advertising, 11,* 27-39.

[13] Werner, C. M., Turner, J., Shipman, K., Twitchell, F. S., et al. (1995). Commitment, behavior, and attitude change: An analysis of voluntary recycling. Special Issue: Green psychology. *Journal of Environmental Psychology, 15,* 197-208.

[14] Pardini, A.U., & Katzev, R.D. (1983-84). The effects of strength of commitment on newspaper recycling. *Journal of Environmental Systems, 13,* 245-254.

[15] Pallak, M.S., Cook, D.A., & Sullivan, J.J. (1980). Commitment and energy conservation. In L. Bickman (Ed.), *Applied Social Psychology Annual* (pp. 235-253). Beverly Hills, CA: Sage.

[16] Wang, T. H. & Katzev, R. D. (1990). Group commitment and resource conservation: Two field experiments on promoting recycling. *Journal of Applied Social Psychology, 20,* 265-275.

[17] Gonzales, M.H., Aronson, E., & Costanzo, M.A. (1988). Using social cognition and persuasion to promote energy conservation: A quasi-experiment. Journal of Applied Social Psychology, 18, 1049-1066.

[18] Stern, P.C., & Gardner, G.T. (1981). Psychological research and energy policy. American Psychologist, 36, 329-342.

[19] Burn, S.M., & Oskamp, S. (1986). Increasing community recycling with persuasive communication and public commitment. *Journal of Applied Social Psychology, 16,* 29-41.

[20] Burn, S.M. (1991). Social psychology and the stimulation of recycling behaviors: The block leader approach. *Journal of Applied Social Psychology, 21,* 611-629.

[21] Kraut, R. E. (1973). Effects of social labeling on giving to charity. *Journal of Experimental Social Psychology, 9,* 551-562.

[22] DeLeon, I. G., & Fuqua, R. W. (1995). The effects of public commitment and group feedback on curbside recycling. *Environment and Behavior, 27,* 233-250.

Chapter 4: Prompts

[1] Gardner, G.T. & Stern, P.C. (1996) *Environmental problems and human behavior.* Boston: Allyn and Bacon.

[2] Geller, E. S., Wylie, R. C., & Farris, J. C. (1971). *An attempt at applying prompting and reinforcement toward pollution control.* Proceedings of the 79th Annual Convention of the American Psychological Association, 6, 701-702.

[3] Smith, J. M., & Bennett, R. (1992). Several antecedent strategies in the reduction of an environmentally destructive behavior. *Psychological*

Reports, 70, 241-242.

4 O'Neill, G. W., Blanck, L. S., & Joyner, M. A. (1980). The use of stimulus control over littering in a natural setting. *Journal of Applied Behavior Analysis, 13,* 379-381.

5 Geller, E. S., Brasted, W. S., & Mann, M. F. (1979). Waste receptacle designs as interventions for litter control. *Journal of Environmental Systems, 9,* 145-160.

6 Luyben, P. D. (1984). Drop and tilt: A comparison of two procedures to increase the use of venetian blinds to conserve energy. *Journal of Community Psychology, 12,* 149-154.

7 Luyben, P. & Cummings, S. (1981-82). Motivating beverage container recycling on a college campus. *Journal of Environmental Systems, 11,* 235-245.

8 Houghton, S. (1993). Using verbal and visual prompts to control littering in high schools. *Educational Studies, 19,* 247-254.

9 Austin, J., Hatfield, D. B., Grindle, A. C. & Bailey, J. S. (1993). Increasing recycling in office environments: The effects of specific, informative cues. *Journal of Applied Behavior Analysis, 26,* 247-253.

10 Schwartz, J. (1990). Shopping for a model community, *Garbage. May-June,* 35-38.

11 To obtain more information about this initiative, contact the Central States Education Center, 809 South Fifth St., Champaign, Illinois 61820, (217) 344 2371.

12 Herrick, D. (1995). Taking it to the stores: Retail sales of recycled products. *Resource Recycling*

13 For additional information regarding the "Get in the Loop - Buy Recycled" campaign, contact: King County Commission for Marketing Recyclable Materials, 400 Yesler Way, Suite 200, Seattle, Washington, 98104, (206) 296 4439, (206) 296 4366 fax.

Chapter 5: Norms

1 Asch, S. (1951). Effects of group pressure upon the modification and distortion of judgment. In M. H. Guetzkow (Ed.), Groups, leadership and men (pp. 117-190). Pittsburgh: Carnegie.; and Asch, S. (1956). Studies of independence and conformity: A minority of one against a unanimous majority. *Psychological Monographs, 70* (9, Whole No. 416).

2 Nisbett, R. E., Borgida, E., Crandall, R. & Reed, H. (1976). Popular induction: Information is not always informative, *Cognition and Social Behavior, 2,* 227-236.

3 Aronson, E., & O'Leary, M. (1982-83). The relative effectiveness of models

and prompts on energy conservation: A field experiment in a shower room. *Journal of Environmental Systems, 12,* 219-224.

[4] Cialdini, R.B., Reno, R.R., & Kallgren, C.A. (1990). A focus theory of normative conduct: Recycling the concept of norms to reduce littering in public places. *Journal of Personality and Social Psychology, 58,* 1015-1026.

[5] Hopper, J. R., & Nielsen, J. M. (1991). Recycling as altruistic behavior: Normative and behavioral strategies to expand participation in a community recycling program. *Environment and Behavior, 23,* 195-220.

[6] Grasmick, H.G., Bursik Jr., R. B. & Kinsey, K.A. (1991). Shame and embarrassment as deterrents to noncompliance with the law: The case of the anti-littering campaign. *Environment and Behavior, 23,* 233-251.

[7] Aronson, E. & O'Leary, M. (1982-83). The relative effectiveness of models and prompts on energy conservation: A field experiment in a shower room. *Journal of Environmental Systems, 12,* 219-224.

Chapter 6: Communication

[1] Stern, P.C., & Aronson, E. (Ed.). (1984). *Energy use: The human dimension.* New York: Freeman.

[2] Gonzales, M.H., Aronson, E., & Costanzo, M.A. (1988). Using social cognition and persuasion to promote energy conservation: A quasi-experiment. *Journal of Applied Social Psychology, 18,* 1049-1066.

[3] Gonzales, M.H., Aronson, E., & Costanzo, M.A. (1988). Using social cognition and persuasion to promote energy conservation: A quasi-experiment. *Journal of Applied Social Psychology, 18,* 1049-1066.

[4] Burn, S.M. (1991). Social psychology and the stimulation of recycling behaviors: The block leader approach. *Journal of Applied Social Psychology, 21,* 611-629.

[5] Kempton, W., & Montgomery, L. (1982). Folk quantification of energy. *Energy, 10,* 817-827.

[6] Kempton, W., Harris, C.K., Keith, J.G., & Weihl, J.S. (1984). Do consumers know what works in energy conservation? In J. Harris & C. Blumstein (Eds.), *What works: Documenting energy conservation in buildings* (pp. 429-438). Washington, D.C.: American Council for an Energy Efficient Economy.

[7] Kempton, W., & Montgomery, L. (1982). Folk quantification of energy. *Energy, 10,* 817-827.

[8] Eagly, A.H., & Chaiken, S. (1975). An attributional analysis of the effect of communicator characteristics on opinion change: The case of communicator attractiveness. *Journal of Personality and Social Psychology,*

32, 136-144.

[9] Craig, C.S., & McCann, J.M. (1978). Assessing communication effects on energy conservation. *Journal of Consumer Research, 5,* 82-88.

[10] Davis, J. J. (1995). The effects of message framing on response to environmental communications. *Journalism and Mass Communication Quarterly, 72,* 285-299.

[11] Lazarus, R., & Folkman, S. (1984). *Stress, appraisal, and coping.* New York: Springer.

[12] McKenzie-Mohr, D., & Dyal, J. (1991). Perceptions of threat, tactical efficacy and competing threats as determinants of pro-disarmament behavior. *Journal of Social Behavior and Personality, 6,* 675-696.

[13] Heckler, S. E. (1994). The role of memory in understanding and encouraging recycling behavior. Special Issue: Psychology, marketing, and recycling. *Psychology and Marketing, 11,* 375-392.

[14] Oskamp, S., Zelezny, L., Schultz, P. W., Hurin, S., Burkhardt, R. & O'Neil, E. (1994). *Commingled versus separated curbside recycling and long-term participation.* Paper presented at the annual conference of the American Psychological Association.

[15] Jacobs, H. E., Bailey, J. S., & Crews, J. I. (1984). Development and analysis of a community-based resource recovery program. *Journal of Applied Behavior Analysis, 17,* 127-145.

[16] Folz, D. H. (1991). Recycling program design, management, and participation: A national survey of municipal experience. *Public Administration Review, 51,* 222-231.

[17] Aronson, E., & Gonzales, M.H. (1990). Alternative social influence processes applied to energy conservation. In J. Edwards, R. S. Tindale, L. Heath, & E. J. Posaval (Eds.), *Social Influences, Processes and Prevention* (pp. 301-325). New York: Plenum.

[18] Bandura, A. (1977). *Social learning theory.* Englewood Cliffs, NJ: Prentice-Hall.

[19] Winett, R.A., Hatcher, J.W., Fort, T.R., Leckliter, I.N., Love, S.Q., Riley, A.W., & Fishback, J.F. (1982). The effects of videotape modeling and daily feedback on residential electricity conservation, home temperature and humidity, perceived comfort, and clothing worn: Winter and summer. *Journal of Applied Behavior Analysis, 15,* 381-402.

[20] Winett, R.A., Leckliter, I.N., Chinn, D.E., Stahl, B., & Love, S.Q. (1985). Effects of television modeling on residential energy conservation. *Journal of Applied Behavior Analysis, 18,* 33-44.

[21] Darley, J.M. (1977-78). Energy conservation techniques as innovations, and their diffusion. *Energy and Buildings, 1,* 339-343.

[22] Darley, J.M., & Beniger, J. R. (1981). Diffusion of energy-conserving innovations. *Journal of Social Issues, 37,* 150-171.

[23] Rogers, E.M., & Shoemaker, F.F. (1971). *Communication of Innovations* (2nd ed.). New York: Free Press.

[24] Burn, S.M. (1991). Social psychology and the stimulation of recycling behaviors: The block leader approach. *Journal of Applied Social Psychology, 21,* 611-629.

[25] Larson, M.E., Houlihan, D., & Goernert, P.N. (1995). Brief report: Effects of informational feedback on aluminum can recycling. *Behavioral Interventions, 10,* 111-117.

[26] Seligman, C., & Darley, J. M. (1977). Feedback as a means of decreasing residential energy consumption. Journal of Applied Psychology, 62, 363-368.

[27] DeLeon, I. G., & Fuqua, R. W. (1995). The effects of public commitment and group feedback on curbside recycling. Special Issue: Litter control and recycling. Environment and Behavior, 27, 233-250.

[28] Rothstein, R. N. (1980). Television feedback used to modify gasoline consumption. Behavior Therapy, 11, 683-688.

Chapter 7: Incentives

[1] Cuthbert, R. (1994). Variable disposal fee impact. *BioCycle, May,* 63-65.

[2] Federation of Canadian Municipalities. A municipal guide on economic instruments to support municipal waste management programs. Toronto, Ontario: Resource Integration Systems Ltd. (RIS).

[3] Recycling Council of Ontario (1996). *Implementing garbage user fees in Ontario.* Toronto, Ontario: Author.

[4] Federation of Canadian Municipalities. (A municipal guide on economic instruments to support municipal waste management programs. Toronto, Ontario: Resource Integration Systems Ltd. (RIS).

[5] Centre & South Hastings Recycling Board (1995). *Blue Box 2000: Breaking 50.* Trenton, Ontario.

[6] Institute of Applied Research (1980). *Michigan litter: After.* Sacramento, California: Author.

[7] Levitt, L., & Leventhal, G. (1986). Litter reduction: How effective is the New York State Bottle Bill?. *Environment and Behavior, 18,* 467-479.

[8] Gardner, G.T. & Stern, P.C. (1996) *Environmental problems and human behavior.* Boston: Allyn and Bacon.

[9] Heberlein, T. A., & Warriner, G. K. (1983). The influence of price and attitude on shifting residential electricity consumption from on- to off-peak periods. *Journal of Economic Psychology, 4,* 107-130.

[10] Heberlein, T. A. & Baumgartner, R. M. (1986). Changing attitudes and electricity consumption in a time-of-use experiment. In Monnier, E. et al., (Eds.), *Consumer behavior and energy policy.* New York: Praeger.

[11] Stern, P. C., Aronson, E., Darley, J. M., Hill, D. H., Hirst, E., Kempton, W. & Wilbanks, T. J. (1985). The effectiveness of incentives for residential energy conservation. *Evaluation Review, 10,* 147-176.

[12] Zuckermann, W. (1992). *End of the road: From world car crisis to sustainable transportation.* Post Mills, Vermont: Chelsea Green.

[13] Hart, S. I. & Spivak, A. L. (1993). *Automobile dependence and denial: The elephant in the bedroom.* Pasadena, California: New Paradigm.

[14] Everett, P. & Watson, B. (1987). Psychological contributions to transportation. In D. Stokols, and I. Altman, (Eds.), *Handbook of Environmental Psychology.* New York: Wiley.

[15] Zuckermann, W. (1992). *End of the road: From world car crisis to sustainable transportation.* Post Mills, Vermont: Chelsea Green.

[16] Geller, E. S., Winnett, R. A., & Everett, P.B. (1982). Preserving the environment: *New strategies for behavior change.* New York: Permagon.

[17] Gardner, G. T. & Stern, P.C. (1996). *Environmental problems and human behavior.* Boston: Allyn and Bacon.

[18] Gardner, G.T. & Stern, P.C. (1996) *Environmental problems and human behavior.* Boston: Allyn and Bacon.

[19] Source unknown

[20] De Young, R. (1984). Motivating people to recycle: The use of incentives. *Resource Recycling, May-June,* 14-15, 42.

[21] Andy Shiller, Capital Regional District, British Columbia, personal correspondence.

CHAPTER 8: REMOVING EXTERNAL BARRIERS

[1] McKenzie-Mohr, D., Nemiroff, L. S., Beers, L., & Desmarais, S. (1995). Determinants of responsible environmental behavior. *Journal of Social Issues, 51,* 139-156.

[2] Zuckermann, W. (1992). *End of the road: From world car crisis to sustainable transportation.* Post Mills, Vermont: Chelsea Green.

[3] Hart, S. I. & Spivak, A. L. (1993). *Automobile dependence and denial: The elephant in the bedroom.* Pasadena, California: New Paradigm Books.

[4] Crosby, L.A., & Taylor, J.R. (1982). Consumer satisfaction with Michigan's container deposit - an ecological perspective. *Journal of Marketing, Winter,* 47-60.

[5] Waterloo Residential Waste Reduction Unit (1992). *Backyard composter/digester participation pilot study.* Waterloo, Ontario.

Quick Reference
Community-Based Social Marketing

When members of a community use resources wisely, for example by recycling or taking mass transit, a community moves toward sustainability. To promote sustainability, then, it is essential to have a firm grasp of how to encourage individuals and businesses effectively to adopt behaviors that are resource efficient.

Most initiatives to foster sustainable behavior rely upon large-scale information campaigns that utilize education and/or advertising to encourage behavior change. While education and advertising can be effective in creating public awareness and in changing attitudes, numerous studies show that behavior change rarely occurs as a result of simply providing information (see Chapter 1). Community-based social marketing is an attractive alternative to information-based campaigns. Community-based social marketing is based upon research in the social sciences that demonstrates that behavior change is most effectively achieved through initiatives delivered at the community level, which focus on removing barriers to an activity while simultaneously enhancing the activities benefits.

Community-based social marketing involves four steps: 1) Identifying the barriers and benefits to an activity, 2) Developing a strategy that utilizes "tools" that have been shown to be effective in changing behavior, 3) Piloting the strategy, and 4) Evaluating the strategy once it has been implemented across a community.

IDENTIFYING BARRIERS
Research indicates that each form of sustainable behavior has its own set of barriers. For example, the factors that impede individuals from composting are quite different from those that preclude more sustainable forms of transportation. Even with apparently closely associated activities such as recycling, composting and source reduction, different sets of barriers and benefits have been found to be important.

Barriers to a sustainable behavior may be internal to an individual, such as one's lack of knowledge, non-supportive attitudes or an absence of motivation. On the other hand, barriers may reside outside the individual, as in changes that need to be made in order for the behavior to be more convenient (e.g., providing curbside organic collection) or affordable (e.g., subsidizing public transit or compost units). Multiple barriers may exist for any form of sustainable behavior. As a result, community-based social marketers begin the development of their marketing plan by identifying these barriers.

Uncovering barriers involves three steps (see Chapter 2). Begin by reviewing relevant articles and reports. Next, obtain qualitative information through focus groups and observation to explore in-depth attitudes and behavior of residents regarding the activity. Finally, conduct a survey with a random sample of residents.

Before conducting a literature review, ensure that you have a clear mandate. That is, you need to know exactly what behavior(s) you are to promote. For example, a mandate to promote waste reduction is too general, while a mandate to promote curbside recycling and backyard composting has the level of detail you need to focus your literature search. In conducting the literature review consult four sources: 1) Trade magazines and newsletters; 2) Reports, 3) Academic articles, and 4) Authors of reports and articles that you found particularly useful.

The literature review will assist you in identifying issues to explore further with residents of your community through focus groups, observation and the surveys. Limit the size of each of your focus groups to 6 to 8 people and make it easy for people to participate by providing services such as childcare and transportation. Come to the focus groups with a set of clearly defined questions that have been informed by your literature review. The facilitator of the focus groups must clearly steer the discussion and ensure that all participants feel comfortable in participating. Have an assistant who takes notes during the group. Don't provide information about your program prior to the focus groups as this information will influence the information you receive from participants. When the focus groups are completed, tabulate the responses that you received and identify barriers that are mentioned by significant numbers of participants.

Focus groups are useful in obtaining in-depth information but are limited by the small number of participants and the influence that the group itself has upon what each member feels comfortable saying. Surveys overcome these two limitations.

Observational studies of specific behaviors are another valuable tool. By directly observing what people do, you can more easily identify skill deficits, sequences and incentives that are already at work to reward existing behaviors. Observational studies help reduce the problems of self-report data and get the researcher much closer to the community and the behavior. Observation is also useful in evaluating behavioral compliance, particularly for behaviors where people are being asked to learn and maintain new skills.

Conducting a survey consists of seven steps.

First, begin by clarifying the objective of the survey. Do this by creating a survey objective statement which indicates the purpose of the survey. This statement can be used to ensure that you have the support of your colleagues before proceeding. This statement can also act as a reference when later deciding upon the relevance of potential survey items.

Second, list the items which are to be measured. Note that at this point you are not concerned with writing the questions, but rather with identifying the "themes" or "topics" that will be covered in the questionnaire.

Third, write the survey. In writing the survey avoid "open-ended" questions since they are difficult to analyze and extend the length of the survey. Further, limit yourself to using only a few types of scales for "closed-ended" questions, as this will speed conducting of the survey. When selecting how many options to provide on the scale, use six- or seven-point scales as they provide a broader range of answers than scales with fewer options. Whether you select six- or seven-point scales, stay with your choice throughout the survey. As you write your survey, ask four questions of each item: 1) Is this a question that can be asked exactly as written?; 2) Is this a question that will mean the same thing to everyone?; 3) Is this a question that people can answer, and 4) Is this a question that people will be willing to answer?

Fourth, when the survey is completed, take the time to pilot it with 10 to 15 people. Piloting the survey allows you to scrutinize the wording of the questions and the length of the survey. Don't include the data you obtain from the pilot with the data you obtain from the actual survey.

Fifth, select the sample. Surveys are most useful when the respondents are randomly selected from your community. A sample has been randomly selected when each adult in the community has an equal chance of being asked to participate. When this criteria is met, you can generalize your results back to the whole community with confidence.

Sixth, conduct the survey. If you are conducting the survey in-house, see the set of instructions for interviewers provided in Chapter 2. If the survey is being conducted for you by a research firm you can expect that it will take approximately a week to two weeks for the survey to be completed.

Seventh, analyze the data. Unless you have someone on staff with a statistical background, you will want to have the survey data analyzed for you. In having the data analyzed, ask for a thorough description of those individuals who are engaging in the activity, as well as for those that are not (descriptive statistics). Also, ask for the factors that distinguish people who are doing the behavior, such as composting, from those who are not, and the relative importance of these factors (multivariate statistics).

Significant pressures, such as time and staffing constraints, and increased project costs often result in this first step, the identification of barriers, being skipped. While these pressures are real and important, failure to identify barriers will often result in a program that either has a diminished impact or no impact at all. The identification of barriers is an essential first step to the development of a sound community-based social marketing strategy. By conducting a literature review, focus groups, observation and a survey you will be well positioned to develop an effective strategy.

TOOLS OF BEHAVIOR CHANGE

Community-based social marketing draws upon research in the social sciences, and particularly psychology, that has identified a variety of effective "tools" for promoting behavior change. Keep in mind that these tools are often most effective when used in combination with one another.

These tools are as follows:

Commitment

In a wide variety of settings people who have initially agreed to a small request, such as to wear a button saying they support the purchase of products with recycled-content, have subsequently been found to be far more likely to agree to a larger request, such as actually purchasing these products.

Why does seeking commitment to an initial small request work? There are likely two reasons. First, when people go along with an initial request, it often alters the way they perceive themselves. That is, they come to see themselves, for example, as the type of person who believes it is important to purchase products that have recycled content. Second, we have a strong desire to be seen as consistent by others. Indeed, our society emphasizes consistency and people who are inconsistent are often viewed negatively. As a result, if we agree to wear a button supporting the purchase of recycled-content products, it would be inconsistent not to purchase these products when we shop.

Commitment as a behavior change tool has been utilized in a variety of studies with often dramatic results (see Chapter 3). In considering using commitment, follow these guidelines:

Emphasize written over verbal commitments. Written commitments have been found to be more effective in bringing about long-term change.

Ask for public commitments: When commitments are made public, such as by having names advertised in a newspaper, behavior change is more likely.

Seek commitments in groups: If possible, seek commitments from groups of people that are highly cohesive, such as a church group. The close ties of these individuals, coupled with the importance of being consistent, make it more likely that people will follow through with their commitment.

Actively involve the person. When people are actively involved — for instance, asked to peer into an attic or hold a container to measure the flow-rate of a shower — they are more likely to see themselves as committed to the activity.

Use existing points of contact to obtain commitments: Wherever natural contact occurs, look for opportunities to seek a commitment. For example, when people purchase paint ask them to sign a commitment that they will dispose of any left-over paint properly, or, better yet, take it to a paint exchange if one exists.

Help people to view themselves as environmentally concerned. We can help people to see themselves as environmentally concerned, and therefore more committed to other sustainable activities, by commenting on their past actions. For example, when someone comes to pick up a composter, ask them if they recycle. If they do, note that their recycling is evidence of their concern for the environment and that beginning composting is a natural way to reduce waste even more.

Don't use coercion. In order for this behavior change tool to be effective, the commitment has to be freely volunteered. That is, only ask for commitments when people appear to be interested in an activity.

Prompts

Numerous behaviors that support sustainability are susceptible to the most human of traits: forgetting. People have to *remember* to turn off lights, check the air pressure in car tires, turn off the engine when waiting to pick someone up, turn down the thermostat, select items that have recycled-content, etc. Fortunately, prompts can be very effective in reminding us to perform these activities (see Chapter 4). Prompts are visual or auditory aids which remind us to carry out an activity that we might otherwise forget. In using prompts you will want to ensure that you follow these guidelines:

Make the prompt noticeable. In order for a prompt to be effective it has to be noticed first. Make sure that your prompt is vivid (a bright color) and eye-catching.

Make the prompt self-explanatory. All the information that is needed for someone to take the appropriate action should be conveyed in the prompt. For example, if you were using a prompt to increase the likelihood that people with odd numbered street addresses would water their lawns only on odd numbered calendar days (and vice versa), the prompt that you attach to an outside faucet could read "water your lawn only on odd numbered calendar days".

Present the prompt in as close proximity as is possible to where the action is to be taken. If you want to encourage people to turn off lights upon leaving a room, for example, affix the prompt beside or directly on the light switch plate.

Use prompts to encourage people to engage in positive behaviors. It is important, when possible, to encourage positive behaviors. If you want people to purchase environmentally friendly products when shopping, place prompts throughout a store that bring attention to those items rather than bringing attention to items that should be avoided. Not only is the encouragement of positive behaviors more likely to be supported by retail outlets (few would let negative prompts be posted), but positive behaviors also make people feel good about their actions, which increases the likelihood that the actions will be carried out in the future.

Norms

To date, few programs have emphasized the development of community norms which support people engaging in sustainable behavior. This lack of attention to norms is unfortunate, given the impact they can have upon behavior (see Chapter 5). Norms guide how we should behave. If we observe others acting unsustainably, for instance using water inefficiently, we are more likely to act similarly. In contrast, if we observe members of our community acting sustainably, we are more likely to do the same.

When considering including norms in programs you develop, keep the following guidelines in mind:

Make the Norm Visible. For norms to influence the behavior of others they have to be aware of the norm. The very act of taking recyclables to the curbside, for example, communicates a community norm about the importance of recycling. Most sustainable activities, however, do not have the community visibility which recycling has, and norms that support the activity, therefore, have to be promoted more actively. Find ways to publicize involvement in sustainable activities, such as providing ongoing community feedback on the amount of water that has been saved by homes using water efficiently.

Use Personal Contact to Reinforce Norms. Research suggests that internalization of norms is more likely to occur as a result of personal contact. As a consequence, use personal contact as an opportunity to reinforce norms that support sustainable behavior.

Communication

All programs to foster sustainable behavior include a communication component. The impact of communications upon behavior can vary dramatically based upon how the communication is developed (see Chapter 6). To develop effective communications, include the following elements:

Use Captivating Information. All persuasion depends upon capturing attention. Without attention, persuasion is impossible. Communications can be made more effective by ensuring that they are vivid, personal and concrete.

Know your Audience. All communications should be developed with your audience in mind. Before developing communications, you should have a firm sense of the attitudes, beliefs and behavior of your intended audience(s).

Use a Credible Source. The individual or organization that presents your message can have a dramatic impact upon how it is received and subsequent behavior. Ensure that whoever delivers your message is seen as credible. Individuals or organizations tend to be viewed as credible when they have expertise, or are seen as trustworthy.

Frame your Message. How you present or "frame" your activity can impact upon the likelihood that people will engage in it. In general, you should emphasize the losses that occur as a result of inaction (e.g., from not insulating) rather than the savings that occur from action (e.g. insulating).

Carefully Consider Threatening Messages. While environmental issues lend themselves easily to the use of threatening or fearful messages, do so with caution. While the public needs to understand the implications of such serious issues as global warming, toxic waste, or ozone depletion, they also need to be told what positive action they can take if threatening information is to be useful. In short, whenever you contemplate using a threatening message consider whether you can at the same time present concrete actions that individuals can take to reduce the threat.

Decide on a One-Sided versus Two-Sided Message. One-sided communications are usually more persuasive with audiences who have little or no comprehension of an issue. As knowledge increases, however, two-sided messages are generally more persuasive.

Make Your Message Easy to Remember. All sustainable activities depend upon memory. People have to remember what to do, when to do it, and how to do it. Use prompts (Chapter 4) to assist people in remembering. Also develop messages that are clear and specific.

Provide Personal or Community Goals. Providing targets for a household or community to achieve can help to provide motivation for sustainable behavior.

Emphasize Personal Contact. Research on persuasion documents that the major influence upon our attitudes and behavior is not the media, but rather the people with whom we interact . Create opportunities for people to talk to one another through programs such as block leaders, in which individuals who already have experience in a sustainable activity, such as composting, speak to others from their neighborhood. Through personal contact, provide opportunities for people to model sustainable behavior for one another, such as installing weather-stripping, and facilitate ongoing discussions in your community to allow social diffusion of new behaviors to occur.

Provide Feedback. Remember to provide members of your community with feedback about the effectiveness of their actions. Feedback has been found to have a positive impact upon the adoption and maintenance of sustainable behaviors.

Incentives

Incentives have been shown to have a substantial impact on a variety of sustainable activities including waste reduction, energy efficiency and transportation. They are particularly useful when motivation to engage in action is low, or people are not doing the activity as effectively as they could. Gardner and Stern (1996) suggest the following guidelines in using incentives:

Closely Pair the Incentive and the Behavior. The closer in time the incentive is presented to the behavior it is meant to affect, the more likely that it will be effective.

Use Incentives to Reward Positive Behavior. Where possible, use incentives to reward people for taking positive actions, such as returning beverage containers, rather than fining them for engaging in negative actions, such as littering.

Make the Incentive Visible. For incentives to be effective, you need to draw people's attention to them. Consider using vivid techniques to make incentives noticeable (see Chapter 6). Also, incentives can be made more visible by closely associating them with the behavior they are meant to effect, such as having people attach tags to their garbage bags in order to have them picked up in a user pay garbage disposal program.

Be Cautious about Removing Incentives: Incentives can be powerful levers to motivate behavior, but they can also undermine internal motivations that people have for engaging in an activity. If you plan to use an incentive to encourage a sustainable behavior, remember that if you elect to remove the incentive at a later time the level of motivation that existed prior to the introduction of the incentive may no longer exist.

Prepare for People's Attempts to Avoid the Incentive. Incentives such as separate laneways for multiple occupant vehicles can have a significant impact upon behavior. However, because these incentives powerfully reward one behavior (car pooling) and strongly punish another (single occupant driving), there is strong motivation to try to "beat" the incentive. In preparing incentives, give careful consideration to how people may try to avoid the incentive and plan accordingly.

Carefully Consider the Size of the Incentive. In arriving at what size of incentive to use, study the experience of other communities in applying incentives to motivate the same behavior.

Use Non-Monetary Incentives. While most incentives are monetary, nonmonetary incentives, such as social approval, can also exert a strong influence upon behavior. Consider ways that social approval and other nonmonetary incentives can be integrated into your program.

Removing External Barriers

The behavior change strategies presented in this book can have a significant influence upon the adoption and maintenance of behavior. However, they will be ineffectual if significant external barriers exist to the behavior you wish to promote. It is important to identify these barriers and plan for how you will overcome them. Study other communities to see how they have managed to overcome similar obstacles. Assess whether you have the resources to overcome the external barriers you identify. If you do not, carefully consider whether you wish to implement a program.

DESIGN AND EVALUATION

The design of a community-based social marketing strategy begins with identifying the barriers to the activity you wish to promote. Knowledge of barriers is particularly important. Without this information it is impossible to design an effective program. In identifying barriers, be sure to conduct statistical analysis that allows you to prioritize the barriers. Knowing the relative importance of barriers will allow you to use limited resources to their greatest benefit. Once you have identified and prioritized your barriers, select behavior change tools that match the barriers you are trying to overcome. When you have arrived at a design for your program, obtain feedback on your plans from several focus groups. Look for recurring themes in their comments as they may indicate areas in which your planned program needs to be redesigned. Once you are confident that you have a program that should affect behavior, pilot the program. In conducting the pilot, ensure that you have at least two groups; one that receives the intervention and another that serves as a comparison or control group. Randomly assign households or individuals into either group to ensure that the only difference between the groups is whether or not they received the intervention. In evaluating the effectiveness of your pilot, focus on behavior change rather than measures of awareness or attitude change. If your pilot is not successful in altering behavior, revise your strategy and pilot it again. Assuming that you know why a pilot did not work, and that you now have the information you need to go straight to community-wide implementation, can be a very expensive mistake. When your pilot is effectively changing behavior you are ready to implement your strategy across the community. Evaluate the community-wide implementation by obtaining information on baseline involvement in the activity prior to implementation, and at several points afterward.

About the Authors

Dr. Doug McKenzie-Mohr is an environmental psychologist who specializes in designing programs to promote sustainable behavior. For the last decade his award-winning work has focused on incorporating scientific knowledge on behavior change into the design and delivery of community programs. As the founder of community-based social marketing, he has repeatedly illustrated its utility in his research, workshops, and consulting. His previous version of this book published through Canada's National Round Table on the Environment and the Economy has become requisite reading for those who deliver programs to promote sustainable behavior.

A professor at St.Thomas University in Fredericton, New Brunswick, Dr. McKenzie-Mohr teaches community-based social marketing, social psychology and survey research methods. He has been awarded the Canadian Psychological Association's "Psychologists for Social Responsibility Research and Social Action Award," and the "Society for the Psychological Study of Social Issues Public Advocacy Fellowship." He has also served with Environment Canada, and is a member of National Advisory Committee of the national social marketing campaign, "SustainAbility."

Dr. William A. Smith is Executive Vice President at the Academy for Educational Development in Washington, DC. Since 1978, he has led the Academy's portfolio of public health communication and social marketing programs working in over 65 countries and focusing on environmental issues, medical and health issues, and AIDS prevention. Dr. Smith has been closely involved in designing and guiding the Academy's work in behavioral research, public health communication, social marketing, and environmental education. He has also been the senior technical advisor to the USAID-funded Environmental Education and Communication (GreenCOM) Project since its inception in 1993.